Advance Praise for *Far from Fine*

As Shwetha says, we sleepwalk through life. To protect us from the ravages of stress and inevitable pain, our brains shut down our ability to be present. We become numb. By the time we are adults, we don't know how to feel joy. Reading *Far from Fine* can wake you up, bringing you back to life. It offers an effective blueprint for personal transformation. With 'Points to Ponder' and 'Self-Discovery' exercises, Shwetha deepens self-awareness and offers practical tools that are easy to adopt. If you follow along, the journey will help you sculpt an intentional life. The book is a timely reminder to stop living life on autopilot and choose to embrace who you are, what you value, and the totality of life.

—Dr Marcia Reynolds
Internationally recognised coach and author of *Outsmart Your Brain* and *Breakthrough Coaching*

As our society has made tremendous progress in the material world, moving a lot of people up on Maslow's hierarchy, the needs of society are shifting to questions around self-actualisation versus questions of food and security. Our past mental models made in the era of scarcity were reasonably simple and deterministic, given the paucity of opportunities and choices. Thus, following the herd or sleepwalking through life was an okay strategy for a large number of people and seems to have certainly worked for me thus far (I was born on the day of the moon landing). However, the world of abundance that now faces many cannot be traversed effectively with the mental models of the scarcity era and provides an opportunity for everyone to create their own unique path. *Far from Fine* provides a comprehensive explanation and lays out the strategy for crafting your own unique path in current times.

—Pankaj Rai
Group Chief Data and Analytics Officer, Aditya Birla Group

A beautiful and much-needed reminder to pay attention to your current state, coupled with actionable steps for personal growth.

—**Derek Sivers**

Author of *Useful Not True, How to Live,* and *Hell Yeah or No*

About 40 trillion cells have come together in an incredibly complex and harmonious dance to give each of us a unique gift—our life. We owe it to ourselves to maximise every moment of our lives, playing to our unique strengths instead of merely existing. This book provides the readers with an easily relatable and remarkably effective blueprint for personal transformation. Shwetha gives us that timely reminder that when we find balance, take the time to know who we truly are, and believe in our capabilities, we can accomplish anything we desire.

—**RamG Vallath**

Bestselling author, motivational speaker, and positive-mindset coach

Don't sleepwalk through your life . . . that would be such a travesty, despite all the accolades that you may have accumulated along the way. Create your own destiny. Bring more meaning and joy into your everyday life. Be more than just fine, and live each moment with great intentionality. These are just a few of the many wonderful pearls of wisdom that you are sure to find in Shwetha's book, which I believe is a much-needed wake-up call for all of us running the corporate rate race.

—**Lulu Raghavan**

Vice President (Asia Pacific), Landor

FAR FROM FINE

A Transformative Journey from Autopilot to Intentional Living

Shwetha Sivaraman

HAY HOUSE INDIA
New Delhi • London • Sydney
Carlsbad, California • New York City

Hay House Publishers (India) Pvt Ltd
Muskaan Complex, Plot No. 3, B-2, Vasant Kunj, New Delhi 110 070, India

Hay House LLC, P.O. Box 5100, Carlsbad, CA 92018-5100, USA
Hay House UK Ltd, The Sixth Floor, Watson House, 54 Baker Street, London W1U 7BU, UK
Hay House Australia Publishing Pty Ltd, 18/36 Ralph St., Alexandria NSW 2015, Australia

Email: contact@hayhouse.co.in
www.hayhouse.co.in

First published by Hay House Publishers India 2024

ISBN 978-81-967512-2-7
ISBN 978-81-967512-7-2 (Ebook)

Printed at
Replika Press Pvt. Ltd.

This book is produced from FSC® paper to ensure responsible forest management.

To Appus & Ammus,
for everything.

Contents

Part III
Beyond Fine

Foreword

Ours is a generation of 'knowledge workers' as predicted by the world-famous management guru, Peter Drucker. It is so true that the highly qualified and super achievers are not really happy. Success does not guarantee calmness, contentment, and happiness. With luxury being the priority, are we all moving to become more comfortably miserable?

Shwetha takes us through this inner journey. In this book, she shares her personal inner thought process and learnings. An achiever and a successful person in her own right, she helps us see the other side of life from a unique perspective. She becomes a mentor and coach and handholds the readers through the process of understanding and realising what is really meant by true happiness through this insightful and timely book. The tips given by her are practical and can be applied by each one of us.

I am sure you will find Shwetha a great guide, the way I found it myself. *Far from Fine* has the power to transform you at a very deep and spiritual level. I wish Shwetha and her book a grand success.

Let all of us achieve true and lasting happiness.

Dr Radhakrishnan Pillai

Author of *Corporate Chanakya* and other Chanakya series books

Director, Chanakya International Institute of Leadership Studies, University of Mumbai

Preface

'I am fine,' 'I am good,' 'I am doing well'; haven't almost all of us said these words with a fake diplomatic smile plastered on our faces on different occasions? We might be crumbling from within, but it's fine. We might not be happy in our relationships, but all is going well. We might be struggling to survive each day, but it is okay. We might be experiencing no joy for weeks, but all is well!

Rarely do we as adults say the truth or mean it when we say we are fine. In fact, it is such an accustomed response that has seeped into our being that we even give the same response to ourselves about how our lives are going. It's going fine! Isn't this how it is supposed to be? I work, earn, and provide for a family, I can't complain.

The truth is that we sleepwalk through our days as mere existence and call it a life. But where is the life in our lives? Most of us are continually stressed and anxious. We toss and turn for hours trying to sleep but to no avail. We intoxicate ourselves with alcohol, drugs, or other substances, hoping that can numb our pain. If that doesn't work, we doom scroll our life away on social media, hoping to vicariously live through other's highlight reels. We feel disconnected and lonely. We lack faith in ourselves. Playing the victim card in every challenging situation. But the important thing that we fail to realise is that by settling for mere existence, we do a great disservice to our abilities, potential, and spirit.

Humans have been around for six million years but over the past few decades, remarkable strides have been made in the material realm, with technological innovations and advancements that have made life so convenient. Yet, we are barely managing to stay afloat. We pretend to be fine, even though dissatisfaction is rife and suffering is the order of the day. However, unlike our ancestors 2,000 years ago, we are not suffering from nature's wrath or lack of access to food or shelter, which is crucial for our survival; this is a different kind of suffering, a self-imposed torment of the mind.

In 2019, a study by the World Health Organization (WHO) revealed that 280 million people were living with depression and 301 million had anxiety disorder, including 58 million children and adolescents. These stats reveal that even though physical suffering is unavoidable in life, the majority of our woes today are mental. That's both empowering and tragic at the same time. Empowering because thankfully, that's something we can actively work towards preventing, healing, and curing, and tragic because we are drowning in our self-created malaise and blaming the world for our miseries.

It is truly unfortunate to be born as a human, one of the most advanced beings on earth, and not experience the full magnificence of life. We are born for greatness. We deserve peace. We deserve happiness. We deserve to move about our daily commitments with ease and contentment. In this brief life, it is crucial to recognise that it's our responsibility to make every moment count, not just someday, but every single day.

This book is written as a wake-up call to remind each of us of our immense potential and what life could be if we dare to stop settling for scraps. A life where we are not the victim of the constant vagaries of the mind. A life where we are not continually gripped by fear and worrying about what tomorrow holds. A life where we are not exhausted all the time and don't wake up each morning with our hearts filled with dread. But where does one break the chain of mere existence to start living and thriving to the fullest? This book hopes to evoke that insight and offer some approaches to getting off that hamster wheel to make intentional life choices.

But before you dedicate the next few hours of your life to this book, it is only fair you first know the author's story.

Lost and Found—
My Homecoming Story

Flowing, in the Wrong Direction

I had an unremarkable childhood, nothing to gaga or boo-boo over. I was born to an average middle-class family and had my share of happy moments and an equal measure of conflict, sorrow, and financial woes. I was a carefree kid, who did what she felt like doing and had the gift of the gab to get away with it for a while. My carefree approach came to a sudden halt by grade ten, and I went from flunking courses to topping classes. Yet, this transition didn't spawn an interest in academics. It was a means to an end to keep people off my back. So, at every juncture, I made decisions based on the principle of minimal discomfort and continued to stride on the path of least resistance.

At fifteen, commerce felt less painful than science. At seventeen, BCom was easier than pursuing chartered accountancy. I pursued MBA entrance exam coaching classes at nineteen because my best friend then wanted to go into an IIM. I was blissfully unaware of such institutions even in 2011. As life would have it, my friend didn't make it, but I did. I walked into XLRI, only to realise it was a rat race I didn't sign up for. Also, being outside the home for the first time at the age of twenty and surrounded by ultra-competitive youngsters from all walks of life, I felt like a ship without a compass, drifting aimlessly in a boundless sea of uncertainty.

It was a moment familiar to many, a phase where we simply go through the motions of life. During this period, I had pretty much forgotten my carefree younger self and my singular focus became to survive. But after a lot of hard work laced with abundant luck, I walked out of campus after two years with a degree, a job at a coveted company, and a potential soulmate.

I arrived in Bombay, the land of dreams, with sufficient education debt to repay. Life in the 'City of Dreams' is hard enough for commoners . . . enough to make you forget larger-than-life questions! You try your best to get through one day at a time. My first few years in corporate India involved working, earning, repaying debt, and spending the remaining money on materialistic things to pamper myself to go back to the job every Monday. The cycle continued, repeating itself in a relentless loop.

I Was Fine, But . . .

My life during this period might have looked brilliant on paper, but I constantly felt something was amiss. I was fine but never truly satisfied. I was fine but could never wake up on Monday mornings with a smile. I was fine but needed to take a vacation every few weeks so that I could continue to function. I was fine but felt like a misfit in every gathering. I was fine but could barely hold it together. I was fine but suffering. And, because I was fine, there was no pressing need to address the discontentment.

I was a high-functioning adult for the world, yet to preserve my sanity, I had to keep taking breaks and travel. It became my escape route, a path that helped me break free from the shackles I imposed on myself unknowingly. It was the space to breathe, expand, pause, and in many ways, realise how this rat race was futile. I unconsciously yearned to reconnect with my past self, and simply be free. The only way to do that was through the drug of travel. Every trip, every destination opened up an old part of me, which I had repressed for years. And each time I returned to the rigmarole of life in Bombay, the urge to travel again took over, driving me to explore one country after another in search of myself.

Soon, I began to notice the difference in my personality during work and travel, leading me to contemplate who I truly was. It became clear that while I did fine in my professional life, it was during my travels that I felt truly alive. And with every trip, the discontentment about going back to being 'fine' became troublesome.

Emergence of the Struggle

Is this it? Is this really it? Existential questions started ringing unabated in my ears. Was this really the life I wanted as an adult? After all, the promises I had heard in childhood—good marks would set me up for a great life of happiness—turned out to be false. My adult life was reduced to a few moments of living when I was far from work and life. It made no sense, and a part of me refused to accept this was it. Though travel soothed the unfulfilling life and heart of mine, the more I escaped, the more disgruntled I became on returning to normal life.

Gradually, I kept dropping more of myself and became mechanical, operating on precision. I suffered panic attacks, even in well-ventilated corporate offices. I would gasp for air, the world seemingly collapsing within my head. I would rush to the elevators in a bid to get out of the building, seeking open spaces in the sheer hope to breathe again.

This went on for many months and, of course, not a soul around me noticed any difference. The machine I had become was still functioning sufficiently well, producing the desired results as a cog in the wheel.

Sprouting of the Seed

The more I asked myself, 'Is this it?', the stronger the answer reverberated within my being was—'This is not it.' My inner child rejected the notion that this was all there was to life. There had to be more to life than just stealing a few fleeting moments of pure bliss untouched by guilt, shame, envy, fear, and regret. It had to be better than a life of constant strife and struggle. Better than a life of seeking continuous escape from reality. Better than a life of playing small and toeing imaginary societal boundaries.

Deep down, I truly believed life could be harmonious, blissful, and filled with loving compassion, no matter the external circumstances. I held the belief that life wasn't a series of obstacles to overcome until retirement brought peace, but rather, a joyride that could be savoured each day, making a living doing what the heart desired.

Somewhere, amidst all this chaos, my brother handed me a book titled *Power of Now* by Eckhart Tolle. I devoured it and could immediately relate; my life was anything but what the book told me life could be.

Ladder of Self-Discovery

I started closely observing my behaviour and thought patterns. This, in turn, prompted me to challenge every aspect of my life—from my actions and choices to my interactions and relationships. Slowly but surely, I came to realise the multitude of unconscious decisions I had made in order to conform to the unspoken expectations of society.

I continued to travel on the side, but a bit more mindfully. It became an exercise to absorb who I was within and without. During one such travel, I experienced the sheer bliss of freedom, and it dawned on me that the time had come to make a change. It was time to walk away from my corporate career and embrace a new path forward.

A Period of Solitude

The ensuing months proved to be the most challenging of my life. Sadly, we have created a world where we can be a subdued version of ourselves in corporate set-ups but not be ourselves, as wholesome humans outside the realm of societal structures. Despite the difficulty, I persevered, doing everything in my power to endure and stay afloat.

By withdrawing myself from the external world, I focused all my attention inward. I travelled, read books, listened to great minds, challenged my limited beliefs, and contemplated life. Day after day, I found myself spending more and more in solitude, gradually shedding layers of insecurity and dismantling false narratives. Also, instead of seeking external opportunities, I paused to ask myself for the first time: What did I want to do? Who did I want to become? What made my heart sing with joy? When did I feel most alive? What did I enjoy doing the most?

As I spent more time with myself, I confronted the uncomfortable truths buried within: insecurities, misplaced self-worth, questions of identity, jealousy, self-doubt, entitlement, disappointment, sadness, and loneliness. These emotions, long repressed and neglected, demanded cleansing and healing.

Self-discovery is often portrayed as a romantic process in movies and social media platforms, but in reality, it's not quite so pleasant. At least not in my experience! It shakes the very foundations of our fragile narratives and makes us question everything. It entails facing the worst parts of ourselves and learning to embrace it with compassion that we have yet to acquire.

Despite the many obstacles, my persistence and willingness to tread the uncharted path led to clarity and deeper awareness. Meditation unlocked a journey of self-discovery, which was nothing short of transcendental. However, I didn't stop there. Driven by an insatiable thirst for knowledge, I continued to seek deeper understanding, which led me to the Indic knowledge systems. Through meditation, learning, and reflection, I peeled back years of conditioning that had burdened me for so many years. Step by step, I made my way back to the core of my being, reconnecting with my true self.

Putting Others before Myself

As my understanding deepened, so did my desire to share my insights with others. Thus, I launched the 'Being Meraklis' podcast to document my journey of learning and self-discovery. However, life had bigger plans for it. The audio journals evolved into a source of profound value for listeners, and the more they resonated, the deeper my own understanding grew.

Over the years, my spiritual exploration continued. Navigating life's demands while preserving my authentic self became my daily endeavour. With much deliberation and effort, I built a life centred on my core values: self-expression, freedom, meaningful work, and conscious community.

Ultimate Surrender

In the past, I was just fine, but now, I simply am. As I walk further along this journey, I am discovering the power of complete surrender, learning to let go and walk the path with unwavering trust in life.

Nowadays, I wake up smiling in gratitude for the blessing of living another day and spend hours before dawn wielding my body and calming my mind. I approach everything with reverence, from the simple act of savouring my morning cup of coffee to receiving early morning hugs from my family, and operate from a quiet sense of certitude, knowing everything is unfolding in my best interest.

I engage with strangers with genuine curiosity, eager to learn more about them and the world around me. Continuously captivated by the awe-inspiring wonders of the universe and life itself, I strive in every moment to grow and evolve without the pressure of reaching a destination. I immerse myself in the wisdom of Indian scriptures and Buddhism, as I am mesmerised by the profound insights our ancestors have preserved so eloquently.

On the whole, I got a glimpse of my true self through a challenging journey and chose to embrace a life of vitality and fulfilment. Motivated by my own experience, I became determined to illuminate the path for others, ensuring they don't stumble blindly through the darkness. This book is a testament to my ongoing journey of learning and sharing. It has taught me invaluable lessons, and I hope that the words within its pages plant seeds of awareness in you, just as another book did for me during my darkest days.

Always remember that freedom, boldness, spontaneity, and vitality are inherent to our existence. As humans, if we cannot embrace these qualities, then what purpose do our intellectual advancements serve? It's imperative to reclaim our birthright by rejecting mere existence—a life dictated by society's norms and expectations. We must design lives that resonate with our deepest selves, igniting our passion and zest for life.

Let this book inspire you to dream big and live boldly, leading lives that surpass even your wildest imagination. We are meant to live extraordinary lives—let's not settle for anything less.

Introduction

'The mass of men lead lives of quiet desperation.'
—Henry David Thoreau

Are you really fine? Your immediate response might be, 'Of course, I am fine. Why won't I be?' But if we probe a little deeper, we would see that most of us are in a bit of a mess and trying our best to stay afloat in the sea of our own suffering. And despite technological advancements and the convenience of the 21st century, we are barely making it from one day to the next and scraping through life. We are either trapped in the past, reminiscing the moments gone by, or dreading the future, anxious about what is to come. Simply put, we are walking on eggshells, barely keeping our sanity on track, as we juggle family, relationships, friendships, career, health, and finances. We find ourselves in a perpetual race, endlessly pursuing something that never quite comes within our grasp. Yet, our standard response remains as: 'I am fine!'

Unconsciously or consciously, we have been conditioned to say these words, no matter what's going on around us or within us. But how did we manage to achieve that conditioning as a collective whole? The upcoming sections will delve into this intriguing phenomenon, shedding light on the origins and implications of our shared conditioning.

It's Me, Not the World

If you were raised in a middle-class family, conservative or not, you would have heard these words more than once: 'Don't wash your dirty laundry in public' or 'Don't expose private matters publicly.'

Social status is very real in our societies. Respect, esteem, and status are values we are wired to seek and value, thanks to our limbic brains. Moreover, our self-worth comes from this status we carry or perceive to carry, and so, we continue placing importance on what society thinks or perceives of us. These evolutionary remnants continue to drive our instinctual need for recognition and validation in society.

In the pursuit of maintaining a respectable and favourable image amidst a so-called educated society, we are raised and conditioned to believe that we are not supposed to discuss problems out in the open. If something is wrong, keep it under wraps! Figure it out in private. The fewer people who know about what you are struggling with, the better. And so, we learn to plaster a diplomatic smile on our faces and walk around portraying a sense of having it all under control; telling, convincing, and projecting to the world that we are merry, happy, jolly, and fine.

Yet, lurking beneath the surface is our sneaky friend, self-doubt, eager to make itself a home in our hearts! This persistent companion raises a few concerns in its tiny but compelling voice: 'If everybody around me seems happy-go-lucky and fine, why can't I be the same way? What if something is wrong with me? Is there anything fundamentally flawed with me that I can't enjoy life as others around me do? Did I miss out on a memo on living the good life that others seem to be navigating so easily?'

Furthermore, the relentless persistence of this internal narrative is magnified by the absence of evidence to the contrary. We don't see our batchmates, peers, or colleagues crumbling from within on their social media feeds. And when no one around us is uttering a word, it is natural to think the problem is with us and not the world. We beat ourselves up and label ourselves as sensitive, anxious, dreamers, wishful thinkers, weak, vulnerable, idealistic, and so on. We wrongly presume that our inability to cope is ours and ours alone and thereby, we suffer in silence.

Adding to the complexity, if we dare speak our minds to somebody, we risk being typecasted. Others start labelling us as too sensitive, too anxious, too prone to stress, and too weak. The fear of being ostracised in society kicks in and so we retreat to our cocoon, pretending all is well because it is easier to go with the tide and follow the herd. We blend in and stop questioning the status quo. And as time passes, it becomes increasingly challenging to maintain the façade, as our energy and courage wane. The longer we persist in pretending everything is fine, the weaker our resolve becomes to tackle real-life challenges. So, we stay safe, succumb to unsaid societal pressures, and continue our world-class act of being fine, while barely getting through the day. We play small and continue to pretend all is well. We convince ourselves this is it . . . this is life. The phrase 'I am fine' eventually becomes a reflexive response, and collectively, we adhere to his unsaid rule and that's the end of the conversation.

Less than One Per Cent

This is the probability of us telling the truth instead of restoring to the automatic response of saying, 'I am fine.' This is the biggest lie we tell the world as well as ourselves every single day, every single moment. We delude ourselves into believing we are fine when the truth is that we are clueless. That we are moving ahead without any knowledge about who we truly are or what we want in this life. We are lost at sea with no anchor to ground us or lifeguards to rescue us. We are out of touch with what's real and what's not and keep going in futile circles with no sense of direction or purpose. Yet, we portray an image of having it all under control. We sleepwalk through life with little to no self-knowledge and unconsciously create an external reality that mirrors the inner muck. We keep busy, distracting ourselves with the many alternatives available to not allow even a single quiet moment, when our inner voice can get through and tell us the scariest four words ever: 'You are not fine.'

And so, we convince ourselves this is how life is. We think it's 'normal' to think compulsively. It's 'normal' to constantly churn the past or worry about the future. We think it's 'normal' to be stressed and anxious all the time. We think drinking and smoking to make peace with our sober lives is 'normal'. We think continuous emotional drama in relationships is 'normal'. We think happiness is the newest hippie fad and that getting through life without joy is the reality.

But is it really? Surely all of us can recall a memory from our childhood where this was not true. A time when being blissfully at peace with ourselves was the norm. A time when the discomfort was fleeting and peace was endless. Stress was momentary and ease was forever. Sadness was temporary and joy was constant. And if you can't recollect your own childhood, look around and observe children. You will notice a vitality in them like no other. They are so full of life that they can keep us raptured for hours. Look at the wonder in their eyes, their inner peace and blissfulness. We were like that too. But we have forgotten that joy and exuberance and have become accustomed to unhappiness and stress.

Conditioning Gone Wrong

We were born as a blank canvas waiting for stories to be imprinted. We soaked in everything from our environment, as it was given to us. At that formative age, we did not question the adults around us. They said our name, we believed it. They said one plus one was two, we believed it. They taught us language, we learnt. Gradually, we kept adding names, colours, objects, emotions, and experiences to this blank canvas, mostly unconsciously. We allowed gradual conditioning to take over and mould us into a weird concoction of all our interpretations of experiences, moving us further away from our inherently blissful state of being.

Our conditioning begins the day we are born. Absorbing every stimulus from our environment—every event, every word spoken or unspoken, every action by those around us: parents, grandparents, relatives, and friends. However, the apex of our conditioning often comes from the education system. Focused solely on intellectual development, it drills us with facts like 'two plus two equals four' and 'the capital of Bangladesh is Dhaka'—facts that, in today's world of readily available information through platforms like Google hold little intrinsic value. This flood of facts leaves hardly any room for introspection and even less space for cultivating internal awareness or self-knowledge.

The truth is that we are spoon-fed answers and are never taught how to think critically. Memory is thc only muscle we flex through our grading systems, and it doesn't help us manage ourselves or our interactions in today's fast-paced world. We have little knowledge about this human body, this mind, and the devious ways in which our minds can work against us despite our best intentions. We are discouraged from understanding our feelings and emotions and walk out of educational institutions emotionally illiterate. Additionally, several years of conventional schooling are more than sufficient to put a stop to the naturally curious parts of us as children. Eventually, we start operating from society's conditioning. After all, it is more than enough to survive.

In the end, our experiences and the narratives we tell ourselves about ourselves, over and over again become our truth, and we soon forget that our true nature was and will remain a blank canvas. The story of 'The Golden Buddha', popularised by author Alan Cohen, captures this aspect of uncovering our inner brilliance perfectly.

In a village in Thailand, there stood a temple that was home to a priceless treasure—the Golden Buddha statue. Many monks took shelter there, tasked with protecting this invaluable Buddha. One day, word came that the feared Mongol armies were invading and plundering wealth from neighbouring towns. The monks deduced it was only a matter of time before the invaders arrived at their village. So, they resolved to do whatever was necessary to protect their Golden Buddha. After much deliberation, they agreed to conceal the shimmering statue with layers of mud and coloured glass, artfully disguising it to appear as nothing more than a common stone Buddha.

As expected, they were soon attacked, and the Mongol army stripped the town of all possessions of even remote commercial value. However, when they came across the now stone-like Buddha statue, they saw no merit in claiming such a worthless artifact. The invaders left, and the villagers slowly regrouped as life settled back into its rhythms. Yet the priceless Golden Buddha remained entombed under those thick, camouflaging layers of mud.

Then one day, some 200 years later, a young monk meditating before the stone Buddha noticed a tiny glimmer of gold that had chipped and fallen by the statue's base. He pointed it out to the other monks, and together they began carefully stripping away the accumulated layers of dirt and dust. To their awe, they gradually uncovered the Golden Buddha in all its radiant glory, still shining as brilliantly as ever centuries after it had been lovingly preserved.

The moral of the story is that there exists an innate brilliance and wisdom buried deep within each of us, beneath the exterior façade of diplomatic and mechanical adulthood we construct. We are all born with an intrinsic knowing, which we gradually hide and obscure as we cover ourselves with layers of metaphorical mud and dust simply to 'fit in' with the conventional ways of the world.

In this magnificent universe, the creator surely did not intend for us to merely function as robotic cogs in the wheels of capitalistic economies. We owe it to ourselves and to the divine spark within to uncover the Golden Buddha, to reveal our inherent radiance from beneath those self-imposed layers of camouflage. It is our spiritual responsibility to do the inquiring, self-examining work to rediscover that brilliant essence at our core. Only then can we make this fleeting human journey truly worthwhile. The Golden Buddha awaits our loving excavation.

Drifting Unconsciously

Somewhere along the journey into adulthood, we start to drift, accumulating that metaphorical mud. We fall into a prescribed rhythm of what is expected of us. Wake up, brush, shower, eat, work, pretend to care, come back home, watch television, guzzle half a bottle of wine, pass out, or in some cases, muster the effort to walk to bed.

We drift through life, mindlessly repeating pattern after pattern. Life begins happening to us on autopilot. We spend our days merely waiting for the weekend, the holidays, the next vacation. The reason we are asleep is that somewhere down that road to adulthood, we found it easier to completely bury the parts of ourselves that made us feel truly alive. We stowed away that magical, spirited being that the world rejected because we couldn't continuously function in contradiction to our free inner nature day after day. Thus began the self-diminishing journey of shunning that voice, that vibrant inner symphony, lulling ourselves into a numb slumber where we become hollow and indistinguishable voids within these bodies because we deny expression to what makes us authentically 'us'.

But if we can awaken from this deep, conditioned sleep we have drifted into, we can catalyse real inner change before hitting rock bottom. We can choose to reanimate that essential aliveness again before it's too late.

Imploding Together and Individually

The world today is on the brink of imploding due to the collectively self-imposed madness we have allowed to go on for far too long. We have been hardwired to engage in the mad chase for material possessions and status symbols, despite their little relevance when it comes to the quality of our lives. We have moved far away from our true nature and imprisoned ourselves in the concrete coffins we call home.

Therefore, it is crucial that we break this vicious cycle of suffering, and this change begins with us—each and every one of us. We need to wake up, shift our gaze inward, and realise that we are not fine. We need to muster the courage to confront our self-sabotaging ways head-on and embark on the path that leads to a better version of our own selves. And once we become more aware and centred, our wisdom will ripple out to those around us and before we know it, the world will have a higher percentage of self-aware, kinder, compassionate, and healed adults. This collective dream is what I hope to co-create with the words that follow in this book.

Believe me, if I can do it, you too can!

Part I
Are You Fine?

1
How Are You, Really?

We know our autopilot response to the question 'How are you?', but how are you really? Ask yourself this question privately in a space where you and no one but you can hear the real answer. Skip the flurry of automated responses—I am alright/good/fine or all well/all good—and simply wait for the genuine answers to surface.

If you pause to ask yourself this question, there is a good chance that you will draw a blank. You might feel uncertain, struggling to articulate your thoughts and experiences. This is because we have been deceiving ourselves about this answer for years, if not decades, so it will take time for the truth to emerge in all its complexity. And even after pondering this question repeatedly, the answers may still be scattered. They could manifest as a mix of diverse thoughts, conflicting emotions, or perplexing next steps. The reality is that the answer to this question is not as straightforward given the intricacies of modern life.

In Denial Mode

Over the years, the question has become a perfunctory social greeting with a standard response. Moreover, after years of claiming that we are 'fine' even though that is not the case, we might be afraid to know the truth ourselves. Consequently, we each develop our own coping mechanism, whether it's denial, comparisons to feel better, hyperfunctioning to compensate, or simply remaining ignorant. The fact is that if we have spent all our lives running away from our true emotions, the prospect of confuting them can be daunting. Deep down, we may recognise the unresolved issues we have buried but feel ill-equipped to address them. Therefore, staying in denial feels safer.

When we try really hard to keep a secret safe, we end up forgetting about it ourselves in a bid to do everything to hide it. A similar sentiment was expressed by renowned author, George Orwell, in his dystopian fiction novel, *1984*: 'If you want to keep a secret, you must also hide it from yourself.' Thus, years of trying to keep the secret that 'we are not fine' concealed has conditioned us to hide the real truth from ourselves. We no longer think we are not fine. On the contrary, we are one hundred per cent sure that we are absolutely fine. No room for doubt. No room for error. Even today, we continue to navigate this awkward path of pretence by rationalising to ourselves that everything is alright.

Avoiding the Reality

For some, avoidance of reality can manifest as hyperfunctioning, i.e., being constantly distracted and restless all through our waking hours. If we are busy all the time, we never have to pause, ask tough questions, or reflect on our choices and actions. We engage in meaningless tasks, anything to keep us away from confronting the reality that something in our lives is amiss. We find ourselves moving from one task to another, never truly knowing if we have lived authentically or achieved our fullest potential, until the end of our days.

Another way by which we evade reality is through the good old-fashioned tactic of ignorance. Only if we know something is wrong or will go wrong, do we seek answers. As long as we are ignorant, nothing needs to be done. Thus, we navigate life with our blindfolds securely fastened, oblivious to the fact that we may not be as fine as we assume.

These aspects of our lives need correction because as long as we are busy or ignorant, we can keep avoiding life's bigger questions and miss out on what it means to be alive.

Alone in Our Loneliness

In a world where everyone continues to proclaim with certainty and confidence that they are fine, it is difficult to stand apart from the crowd and say, 'I am not.' But why is it so? We need to understand that one of the primary human needs is to feel a sense of belongingness, to feel seen and heard in a community, and to be accepted by them. Thus, when we have all willingly or unknowingly agreed to a standard response, it's hard to speak 'our' truth, and we find ourselves wondering: 'Would anyone understand me?', 'What if it's just me and the others are truly fine?', and 'What if something is wrong with me?'

As mentioned earlier, it's challenging to override years of conditioning that drive us to seek acceptance and not stand out against the collective. So, we consent to the opinion of the majority and meekly say we are fine too, regardless of our true feelings. The reality is that this experience is universal; everyone has felt this way at some point. Yet, because people rarely share their true feelings, thcy are kept under wraps and remain there. And so, we find ourselves all alone in our loneliness when we can overcome it collectively, supporting and comforting each other through life's highs and lows.

Signs that We Are Not Fine

Now let's look at some tell-tale signs that indicate we are not genuinely fine.

1. **Low Energy**

   A classic sign of not being fine is being low on energy. Nothing excites us much. We constantly feel drained and exhausted while going through the routine. Each day starts to feel the same and we are continually dragging ourselves from one day to the next.

   When we are genuinely fine, there is no room for low energy. There is a profound realisation of our own mortality and that each day we wake up is a blessing in itself! And because of it, we meet every moment with such intensity that it's infectious, uplifting not only ourselves but also those around us.

2. **No Joy or Satisfaction**

   When we are not truly fine, we lose sensitivity towards our emotions in order to avoid negative feelings, such as sadness, anger, despair, and sorrow. However, when we numb the mind, we also close the doors that lead to joy, satisfaction, and pleasure. This is because both positive and negative emotions are interlinked and saying no to one also means rejecting the other! So, when we live life desensitised, hiding behind the façade of being fine, no joy or satisfaction can penetrate our being. And even when it manages to do so, it is fleeting at best and not lasting.

When we are genuinely fine, we allow ourselves to feel all emotions deeply and not get carried away with them. We can feel joy and love as well as sadness and heartbreak and still remain centred. We feel no need to ignore any emotion, pleasant or unpleasant, because we are in control of our response. In short, when we become truly fine, we can process our emotions consciously and live our best life without living in a cocoon.

3. Blame Life

There is a common pattern among sleepwalkers; they exhibit a tendency to dwell on past events or circumstances, attributing their current situation solely to external factors rather than taking ownership of their actions or decisions. Simply put, life happens to them. This recurrent pattern of focusing on external events hinders their ability to enact positive change in their lives. By failing to acknowledge their own agency and responsibility, they may perpetuate a cycle of victimhood and hamper personal growth and development.

In a genuinely fine state, we are fully alive and present, rather than passive observers on the sidelines. We are conscious co-creators, actively engaged in our lives, and make proactive choices aligned with our core beliefs and value systems. We are the architects of our lives and not a victim of circumstances. This does not mean nothing wrong ever happens; instead, we develop the capacity to face adversity with equanimity, embracing both the joys and struggles that come our way as integral parts of the human experience. Life starts to happen for us.

4. **Endless Triggers**

When we are fine only superficially, the smallest of events can trigger us. Whether it's our partner glancing at their phone during a conversation, a passerby wearing a frown, or a boss ignoring us at work, these seemingly insignificant occurrences have the power to trigger strong emotional responses within us. In this state, we find ourselves riding an emotional rollercoaster, with each twist and turn amplifying our feelings of instability and unease.

Thus, we can see that not being in control of the mind and going through continuous mood swings—swaying with each thought and feeling the monkey mind generates—is a classic sign of not being fine. On the other hand, when we are genuinely fine, we are aware enough to decide which thoughts can enter the perimeter of our minds. We can harness that tranquillity within, unaffected by the storms brewing all around us. Whether our bosses smile or yell, we are at peace. Whether we see that adorable dog on our way to work or not, we are at peace. Whether we are stuck in traffic or not, we are at peace. Whether our partner surprises us or not, we are at peace. Whether our kids call us or not, we are at peace. Whether we make a million dollars or not, we are at peace.

5. Lack of Purpose

When we are merely fine, there is no compelling force driving us forward. We follow a monotonous routine, repeating the same motions day in and day out, often without considering the broader context of our existence. Caught up in the trivialities of daily existence, we overlook the profound beauty and significance of each moment. Unaware of how our actions shape the grand tapestry of life, we remain oblivious to its magnificence.

When we are truly fine, we are fully immersed in life and remain deeply connected to our purpose. It acts as a catalyst, propelling us forward every moment of every day. Our larger-than-life purpose excites us to jump out of bed every morning to do the task at hand with everything we have got. With one eye on the big picture, we realise that every action holds significance and contributes to our greater cause. Thereby, each endeavour, no matter how small, is infused with meaning and brings us closer to fulfilling our purpose.

6. Pessimism

When we are not fine, pessimism and cynicism set in. Our passive approach to living leads us to believe that there is not much to life. We convince ourselves that it is something that needs to be endured and we don't do anything actively to change it at all. We resign to our fates and let it play out, without attempting to course-correct. Our thoughts and beliefs become self-fulfilling prophecies and we get stuck in the vicious circle of pessimism, which becomes more insidious with each unfavourable situation.

When we are genuinely fine, we are proactive and filled with zest that makes us want to strive for improvement. Optimism then becomes the natural way of life. We embrace hope and eagerly anticipate what the future holds, knowing that we play an active role in shaping our own destiny. This proactive mindset becomes second nature to us, driving us to seize opportunities, overcome challenges, and create the life we desire.

7. No Sense of Play

When we are 'fine,' everything about life becomes serious. It requires all our energy to maintain this level of functioning, leaving no room for playfulness or enjoyment. Life feels solemn and serious and leaves us with little capacity to cope with additional hardships.

Playfulness and joy are a natural way of life when we are genuinely fine. Being connected with our inner spirit, we perceive beauty in every moment and thereby, life loses its seriousness. We take each day as it comes and remain immune to self-inflicted miseries. We choose what affects us and what does not. We are also able to navigate life with ease and a sense of play guiding our thoughts, feelings, and actions. The ego takes a backseat, allowing us to be humble and surrender to the creator and the ways of creation.

Points to Ponder

Here are 7 self-introspection questions to self-assess how fine you really are:

1. In the last 7 days, how many times did you experience high energies?
2. In the last 7 days, how many times did you feel genuinely happy or content?
3. In the last 7 days, how many times did you proactively choose what you would like to engage in instead of going with the flow?
4. In the last 7 days, how many times were you able to keep your cool without being triggered by people or situations around you?
5. In the last 7 days, how many times did you feel fully aligned and purposeful?
6. In the last 7 days, how many times did you wake up looking forward to the day?
7. In the last 7 days, how many days did you go about your usual daily routine with a sense of light-heartedness and playfulness?

For each question, if your answer is four or less, it's probably time to reassess how you are really doing. But fret not as we will embark on this journey of becoming fine together. Before that, let's better understand the many ways we are not as fine as we proclaim.

2

You Are Fine, Just Stressed

We proudly wear being stressed as a badge of honour in current times as it implies that we are doing something important. Many would even say that we don't qualify as being adults if we are not stressed. But constant stress takes a toll on our bodies, robs us of peace, and wrecks our quality of life. We feel more exhausted when we get no respite from stress and all our bodily functions go for a toss. Being in overdrive all the time can also dull our mental sharpness. Eventually, chronic stress can even manifest into life-threatening consequences.

Before we delve into methods to alleviate stress, it's important to grasp the intricacies of stress and its impact on our well-being.

Decoding Stress

Simply put, stress is a response to a real or perceived threat. The important takeaways here are that stress is a response—our response—to a 'stressor' or a trigger, which could be people, circumstances, or simply our own minds. The trigger could be a real threat like a tiger chasing us or an imagined situation in the mind, when we let our thoughts or fears wander too far. Regardless of whether the stressor is real or imagined, the response is always real, which, in turn, impacts us physically, biologically, and physiologically. In other words, we experience the response in our body and mind.

There are four dimensions to a stress response:

- A trigger: The event or the stressor that is the cause of the reaction.
- A negative appraisal of the trigger: We are not stressed when favourable events happen. We are stressed only when we appraise the trigger to be unfavourable to us in some way.
- Stress is the response: Our response to the negative appraisal of the situation translates to physical, emotional, and physiological changes. We get tense, angry, frustrated and react impulsively, while physiologically the body goes into a 'fight or flight' mode.
- Return to baseline: We don't remain in that 'fight or flight' mode. Once the trigger passes, our response comes to a natural end and we return to our baseline mode of operation.

Think of a deer being chased by a tiger. When it realises the tiger is out to hunt, it becomes completely alert. With fully dilated eyes and adrenaline pumping in its veins, the deer goes into flight mode to escape the predator. But once it outruns the tiger and manages to escape, there is a return to baseline. Meaning, its heart rate comes back to the resting rhythm and its eyes are no longer fully dilated. Then the deer goes back to grazing as if nothing happened.

Now let's look at what happens within our bodies when we are stressed. It all starts with the stressor that activates the stress response in us. The stressor causes an emotional disturbance that triggers the emotional processing centre in our brains—the amygdala. It sends a distress signal to the hypothalamus which is the command centre in the brain that controls involuntary functions in the body like breathing, heartbeat, and blood pressure. The hypothalamus activates the sympathetic nervous system by sending signals through the autonomic nerves to the adrenal glands. The sympathetic nervous system controls our fight-or-flight or freeze response. The activation of adrenal glands leads to the discharge of the hormone epinephrine (also known as adrenaline) within the bloodstream. The epinephrine circulates through the body and brings about several physiological changes, such as a faster heartbeat, an increase in pulse and breathing rate, more oxygen being pushed to the brain to increase alertness and sense perception, and more blood being pushed to our limbs, muscles, heart and other vital organs to give us strength to fight. It is said that the amygdala and the hypothalamus start this even before our visual centres manage to grasp or register what's going on.

As epinephrine subsides, the HPA (hypothalamus, pituitary, and adrenal glands) axis gets activated. The HPA axis continues sending signals to keep the sympathetic nervous system or the 'fight, flight, or freeze' mode on. If the perception of a threat continues, the hypothalamus activates hormonal signals to release cortisol that helps the body remain on high alert. Once the threat passes, cortisol levels fall and the parasympathetic nervous system, or the rest and digest mode, gets activated, which dampens the stress response.

From the above example, we can see that stress is simply a biological function installed within us by default to preserve ourselves. Our response to short-term stress is necessary for our survival. Without this response, we cannot jump off the road when there's an approaching speeding vehicle or cover our heads instantly when we notice something dropping from the ceiling. These are inherent survival instincts that help us stay alive.

Things go from good to worse when we fail to turn off that stress response internally and return to baseline. When our stress response gets activated continuously and we experience chronic stress, the HPA axis remains activated, releasing cortisol continuously while no restorative functions are happening in the body, which impacts us in the long run. This has become a global phenomenon leading to a major health crisis everywhere. But how is it possible that something essential to our existence can evolve into a significant obstacle to our health and happiness? Let's look into this.

When a deer is being hunted by a tiger, its stress response gets activated for a clear objective: to survive. All its bodily resources are optimised and geared only towards that primary goal. That means when the stress response is on, no cells are being repaired, no organs are detoxing, etc. Basically, all general functions of the body are kept on hold as the body is gearing up for a fight. However, once the objective is achieved, the body restores all its regular functions. The issue arises when the body remains constantly in stress mode and is not able to return to its baseline functioning. And the reason for this is that in the current times, our minds are being constantly bombarded with information from all corners due to which our stress response is always on. We continuously perceive threats, real and imagined, and stay in a state of chronic stress, never allowing the body to hit the brakes and activate the parasympathetic nervous system. And when the body continuously remains in the state of fight, flight or freeze, we are using up resources at a much faster rate and allowing no time for rest. Additionally, when we are constantly stressed, sleep is the first casualty, taking away the only other opportunity the body has to rest and replenish.

Over time, chronic stress can lead to physical as well as psychological consequences, such as headaches, muscle pains, fatigue, mental issues like anxiety, restlessness, irritability, behavioural changes, addiction to substances, extreme mood swings, and lack of motivation or focus.

Failing to See the Bigger Picture

When we are stressed all the time, all our energy, focus, and attention are narrowed to that one single threat or issue we are obsessing about. We zone in on that single mistake or that one thing that didn't go in our favour and convince ourselves that it is the end of the world. But is that the case?

Surely, we all have given bad presentations, failed an exam, or made some mistakes but still managed to do well for ourselves. We all have been stressed about something in the past, which over time feels silly and redundant.

The truth is that the thing which is most important in life is life itself! So, as long as we have a beating heart, lungs full of oxygen, a sane mind, and an able body, we can still do something and make the most of this life. Yet, we pay no attention to this all-important 'life'. We place undue importance on our work, relationships, status, and wealth and spend our precious time worrying about what will happen to us if they go away tomorrow.

In Bhaja Govindam, Adi Shankaracharya eloquently captures the folly of human beings fixating on the trivial while neglecting what truly matters in the following verse:

बालस्तावत्क्रीडासक्तः
तरुणस्तावत्तरुणीसक्तः ।
वृद्धस्तावच्चिन्तासक्तः
परमे ब्रह्मणि कोऽपि न सक्तः ॥

The verse translates as follows:

As a child, we are attached to toys. Stress is induced when someone takes away the most precious possessions at that age, the toys. As adolescents, we are attached to other young people and stressed about anything that ruins our sense of belonging. As we age, we become attached to our worries of tomorrow. And amidst all this, no one is focusing on that one supreme reality.

Though some of us may not be spiritually inclined to focus on Supreme Brahman, we all could do with a shift in perspective on what's really important in our lives. It would help us let go of the undue stress regarding not-so-important things. Instead of attaching inordinate meaning and importance to trivial things, we could consciously stay connected with the true nature of our lives.

All in all, life is uncertain. We do not know what can happen to us in the next moment and that is our reality. We can keep trying to control all aspects of our lives so that we never have to confront this harsh truth, but inevitably, it becomes unavoidable. We might as well come to terms with the fact that our future is unknown and uncertain and may not always pan out as we hope. This is simply a fact of life.

A poem, titled *Peace of Wild Things* by Wendell Berry, encapsulates this aspect of life beautifully:

When despair for the world grows in me,
and I wake in the night at the least sound,
in fear of what my life and my children's lives may be,
I go and lie down where the wood drake rests in his beauty on the water,
and the great heron feeds,
I come into the peace of wild things,
who do not tax their lives with forethought of grief,
I come into the presence of still water,
And I feel above me the day-blind stars,
waiting with their light. For a time,
I rest in the grace of the world, and am free.

Wendell Berry highlights that other living beings have a freedom within them; an innate ability to stay present, without worrying about the past or future. They see a threat and do what's needed, but there's no residue of anxiety, grief, or worry. There's only presence . . . complete and unwavering presence. And though humans are blessed with the powers of memory and foresight, if wielded incorrectly, the same powers become a curse. Our memory keeps us anchored to the past, while our imagination goes wild and foresees not one but endless threats in our future. Both render us paralysed from action and out of touch with reality. Realising that no living being on this planet knows what comes next and accepting the unknown is one of the first ways to be genuinely fine. The only thing within our grasp is this brief, now moment.

Unpacking all the baggage of what has happened or what will happen in this transitory life can remove the heavy burden we carry on our shoulders and allow some room to move through life with some ease as well as grace.

Points to Ponder

Stress is not all bad! What's important is to learn to turn off the stress response and come back to a state of resourcefulness. Take a moment to self-assess how stressed you feel on a scale of 1 to 10 (10 being extremely stressed)? What are some ways you can adopt to remind yourself of what's truly important to turn off that stress response and return to baseline?

3

You Are Fine, but Numb

Have you noticed how people who keep repeating they are 'fine' have little or no emotion? They are more like robots, mechanical in their ways, conversations, and actions. The crispness of the morning air, the smell of earth after it rains, the sight of a rainbow or a striking sunset, nothing evokes any emotion in them. They also pretend as if they feel no pain, hurt, shame, or any unpleasant emotions. All circumstances and events of life seem the same to them.

This phenomenon happens unconsciously when we shun ourselves from feeling anything over several years. The classic accusation made by Joey to Chandler from the famous popular sitcom *F.R.I.E.N.D.S.*, 'You're dead inside,' perfectly captures this sentiment.

People develop all kinds of coping mechanisms to deal with their environments. And when you are in an environment where hurt, anger, fear, and dissatisfaction are prevalent emotions, it can become quite difficult to navigate life while constantly feeling such unpleasant emotions. So, to survive, we start numbing ourselves, as we want to avoid pain at all costs. It becomes our defence mechanism to cope with the never-ending pains and pressures of the modern world.

But when we avoid pain, we also avoid pleasure. That's just the way nature works. It doesn't discriminate between pleasant and unpleasant emotions. Simply put, you cannot have one without the other. So, when we numb ourselves, we also stop feeling love, joy, gratitude, and all other positive emotions. This is also the reason why numbing is a coping mechanism and not a healing mechanism.

Moreover, contrary to popular belief, numbness is not a consequence of indifference; rather, it's a combination of caring too much and fear. Before we build coping mechanisms to numb our surroundings, the truth is that we are naturally sensitive to the people around us and our environment. However, when this sensitivity is constantly exposed to pain, hurt, and distress, we begin to numb ourselves. It became easier to avoid feeling anything than to endure such intense emotions. Thus, we become impervious to everything life has to offer and adopt a state of 'fine' by numbing ourselves from experiencing any emotion.

This strategy works to a large extent, but only for some time. By numbing ourselves from feeling anything, we maintain a facade of stability as we navigate the logical and rational external world. This approach allows us to attain success in the material world by keeping everything below the surface and diplomatically wading through life. But we cannot keep this act up for long. Slowly, but surely, the weight of the unfelt feelings starts to burden us. We feel more and more resistance to carry on with the pretence because everything is not fine. Thus, when we cope by numbing ourselves, we accumulate feelings from every interaction and life experience, leaving them unprocessed for extended periods which eventually leads to an outburst.

To illustrate this concept further, let's consider the following analogy I came across during my journey of healing. Imagine each feeling as a type of fruit. Every life experience elicits an emotional response, shaped by our individual worldview, interpretation, and meaning attributed to it. We can liken each feeling to a specific fruit; for instance, joy could be represented by oranges, sadness by grapes, excitement by dragon fruit, and disappointment by papaya. As time passes and we accumulate various life experiences, it is reasonable to assume that we hold within us a basket of fruits representing our emotions, gathered over the years. However, when we numb ourselves, we continuously add to this basket without ever processing its contents. Consequently, these emotions stagnate and decay, forming a concoction of foul-smelling fruits within us. These unprocessed feelings act as a poison, affecting us from within.

The healthy way to be emotionally stable is to eat the fruit, i.e., feel it, process it, and then discard it immediately. But most of us don't do that. We wait until we cannot tolerate the stench of rotting fruit (complicated unprocessed emotions) within us. At this stage, differentiating between individual fruits becomes increasingly difficult. Meaning, that emotions bunch up and make it challenging to understand the root cause or identify effective means of addressing them.

Embrace Emotional Authenticity

To feel genuinely fine, we need to stop numbing ourselves and find a healthy way to experience, process, and resolve difficult emotions. We cannot live our best lives by being impervious to life; we can only do so by being sensitive to life and engaging with it wholeheartedly. Simply put, to live fully, we must embrace our humanity, experiencing life with depth and sensitivity, rather than numbing ourselves to it.

While it may feel risky to embrace sensitivity in a world that can be harsh, it's important to recognise that, like a delicate flower facing the wind, vulnerability is a necessary part of growth. A seed may be safer than a blooming flower, but it lacks the beauty and richness of experience. Similarly, it takes courage and strength to allow ourselves to feel deeply, yet it is this vulnerability that adds depth and meaning to life.

If we have spent a long time avoiding certain emotions, it can be challenging to navigate them on our own. In such cases, seeking support from a mental health professional can be beneficial, as they can provide guidance and assistance in untangling complex emotions. Ultimately, to experience true joy, bliss, and peace, we must allow ourselves to feel fully and authentically, which means letting go of the habit of numbing ourselves to life's experiences.

Points to Ponder

Understanding your emotions is vital to experiencing life to the fullest. Learn to sit with your basket of fruits aka emotions, and ask yourself what feelings have you denied yourself from experiencing? If you were to disentangle and process them, what possibilities would open up?

4

You Are Fine, but Have Bad Relationships

One of the fundamental aspects of being human lies in our relationships and how we engage with the world around us. The manner in which we nurture these essential connections can significantly impact the overall quality of our lives.

Indeed, life is a complicated web of interdependent variables, and attaining our utmost potential requires finding a harmonious balance across numerous dimensions, with our relationships being of utmost importance. When this equilibrium is disrupted, it can profoundly affect our physical, mental, and emotional well-being.

Our relationships shape the very fabric of our existence, determining the richness of our daily experiences and the fulfilment we derive from life. Several relationships play pivotal roles in shaping the quality of our lives. How we relate with others, how we relate with key aspects of the world like finances, food, and of course the most crucial of all, how we relate with ourselves.

Relationship with Others and Ourselves

As social beings, we are deeply intertwined with the people we surround ourselves with and with whom we share this precious gift of life. We relate to other people based on our inferences from childhood experiences. Whatever we learn from the dynamics of our relationships while growing up, we put that into practice in adulthood. When we approach others with contempt, we ruthlessly decide for them that they know nothing, and we know better. We feel better off than others and constantly feel disappointed that no one lives up to our standards. Whereas the truth is that only when we are insecure within do we feel better about ourselves by putting others down. We keep others cordoned off at a distance so they can never figure out the emptiness we live with.

When we constantly doubt ourselves or our self-worth, we tend to put others on a pedestal. The underlying thought process here is 'I am not good enough'. When we feel we are not good enough, we go above and beyond to compensate and make up for it. We stretch, overextend, and push ourselves to be there for the other person, and if that's not reciprocated, there is resentment, anger, and frustration. Additionally, the toxicity in our relationships mirrors the relationship we have with ourselves within, and it directly impacts the quality of our lives because it is a primary need for humans—to be seen, to be heard, to simply belong. When we don't relate well with others, there is a void created within us that can never be satiated. We feel lost and lonely; no number of successes accomplished, milestones achieved, wealth created, or possessions amassed can make up for it.

On the other hand, when we unconditionally accept ourselves for who we are, we can extend the same unconditional love in our relationships. Then there is no need for pretence. We show up without fear or contempt, without overcompensating or overshadowing. We relate with others similarly, as equally blessed creations, equally loved by the creator. We see the light in others just as others see the light in us. Such acceptance comes from a deeper place of presence, joy, bliss, and connection to that oneness in the entire universe.

Relationship with Other Aspects of Life

Our relationship with food gives an intriguing insight to our relationship with ourselves. Do you eat to feel better? Or do you purge to reduce the guilt and shame? Both extremes lead to an imbalance and drain our precious life energies. Some of us have an emotional dependency on food. We eat when we are sad, we eat when we are stressed, we eat when we are angry, we eat when we are lonely, we eat when we are depressed, and we eat when we are elated. Food substitutes and fills any void we might have when we are supposedly 'fine'.

Some might have the opposite relation with food—that of aversion. Food is treated as the enemy. If we eat even a little bit, we purge right away, straining ourselves to move it out of our systems. When we consume food with aversion, the aversion stays rooted in our bodies even after the food is eliminated from the system. Aversion to food is an aversion to life. This can come from low self-worth or self-esteem, leading to a feeling that we don't deserve food or taking up society's expectations to look or be a certain way. When we have this aversion to food, we also have an aversion to taking care of or nourishing ourselves.

When we are truly fine within, we have a harmonious relationship with our food. We look at food for what it is—a source of life energies. We treat it gently, don't abuse our bodies, and are grateful for what's on our plate. We consider food as a way to nourish our bodies and our minds to operate at higher levels of efficiency. Food is not used to compensate for our emotional deficiencies, rather it helps us mindfully balance our inner self.

Another significant part of our material survival is money, and how we relate to money also is linked to our sense of self-worth and acceptance. Some of us spend all our money as soon as it hits our accounts, while others are penny-savers who limit every outflow to save for the rainy day, forgetting to live in the process. Some of us believe we can earn money only if we work hard while others believe money and happiness are mutually exclusive.

The important thing to recognise here is that whatever we believe is our reality! If we believe we don't deserve to have sufficient balance in our account, no matter our income levels, we will squander it all away as soon as it finds its way to us. If we believe there is never enough money to secure our future, we will keep earning and saving and will continue to want more without ever living life or enjoying that money. If we believe money can be earned only when we work hard, earning will be tedious. Wealth creation will involve lots of sacrifices, and we will think others around us are lucky because they don't need to work as hard as us to earn their money. Or if we believe money and happiness cannot co-exist, our fear of money will ensure we never have enough if we desire happiness. If we desire money, our fear of losing it will keep happiness elusive.

The truth is that the quality of our relationship with money, food, and the world around us is highly dependent on the type of relationship we have with ourselves. When we nurture love, trust, and compassion within ourselves, we naturally radiate these qualities to others. Likewise, when we hold ourselves in high regard with respect and self-esteem, we naturally extend the same regard to those around us. Deep self-understanding and a strong connection with our true selves empower us to authentically relate to others without needing external guidance. Simply put, when we prioritise improving our relationship with ourselves, we unlock the ability to relate to others and the world authentically and powerfully.

The Most Important Relationship: Your Relationship with Yourself

Most of us who are 'fine,' don't quite have a good relationship with the self. We sabotage our lives because we feel we don't deserve happiness and success yet. On a physical level, we eat unhealthy food, smoke, and drink, despite knowing it is bad for us. We hardly pause to care for ourselves. We know the importance of physical activity and exercise, yet often struggle with finding the energy or motivation to prioritise it in our daily lives. We know our bodies need eight hours of sleep, but instead, we binge-watch the latest Netflix show and end up showing up at work with red eyes and a throbbing headache.

On a mental level, our self-talk can be merciless. We constantly critique ourselves and battle self-doubt and imposter syndrome. We judge ourselves harshly when we can't meet the impossible goals that we had set for ourselves. Our self-criticism knows no bounds, and we crucify ourselves for making mistakes. We describe ourselves with many negative labels that we would dare not use even for our worst enemies.

On an emotional level, we hold ourselves in very low esteem and feel we don't deserve anything good in our lives. Our self-worth hinges on the opinions of others. We subject ourselves to self-deprecation and guilt every time we prioritise our needs. We stress ourselves about what others said and how we could have retorted. We feel shameful for enjoying anything in life. We feel displeased with ourselves, whether we give too much or too less.

To summarise, we are continually perpetuating the cycle of self-hatred and every aspect of our lives is clouded by self-criticism and emotional turmoil. Our thoughts, feelings, and actions are always working against us, and we wonder why our lives are not as beautiful or picture-perfect as the highlight reels and images we keep seeing on social media.

This leads us to the question: How can we expect fulfilment in our lives when our relationship with ourselves is so dysfunctional? The important thing we need to realise is that how we treat ourselves reflects in every aspect of our lives. When we demean ourselves and harbour feelings of unworthiness and self-doubt, our lives stagnate in a state of resentment and fear. Conversely, when we foster a healthier relationship with ourselves, characterised by self-compassion and kindness, we extend these virtues to others.

Hence, the primary relationship we must prioritise and nurture is the one with ourselves. We need to be our own best friend in this process of self-actualisation. We need to show unconditional love towards ourselves in every situation—the good, bad, or ugly. We need to have trust in ourselves, our capabilities, and our skills. We must accept ourselves for all that we are including our flaws and strengths, not-so-good and good aspects, and unpleasant and pleasant things about us. We need to generously forgive ourselves for our mistakes and see how we can learn from them. We need to work with ourselves to become better versions and not be our worst enemy and sabotage ourselves from ever progressing.

Points to Ponder

How we relate with ourselves define how we relate with others and the world around us. Look around you and introspect how your inner self-relationship is reflected in your external relationships? Ask yourself, how can you compassionately nurture yourself and be your best friend?

5

You Are Fine, but Afraid

A dominant aspect that prevents us from being genuinely fine is fear. We are afraid of being exposed for our shortcomings. We are afraid that we might fail. We are afraid that we are going to lose a loved one. We are afraid we might lose our status in society. We are afraid we might never be understood. We are afraid that we might lose it all. We are afraid that we might never find true love. We are afraid time is slipping away. We are afraid that we might never truly live.

In this chapter, we delve deep into the concept of fear, examining its various facets and understanding its profound impact on our lives. Through close examination, we explore how fear manifests in different aspects of our existence and discuss strategies for overcoming its hold on us.

Fear: A Pervasive Challenge in Modern Life

Fear is an emotional state that we find ourselves entangled in as a response to a perceived danger. This danger could be real or imagined, physical or psychological, but it triggers the same high emotional response. This response causes an imbalance in our minds, which influences how we think, feel, and act. Over time, these responses become ingrained in us and shape the very core of our sense of self.

For some of us, excessive fear could be a result of an underlying medical condition. But for many of us well-exposed and functioning adults, fears come from our wild imagination and incessant thoughts. Being true to our generation that relies on logic for everything, most of us have an innate tendency to overthink while seeking solutions. There's nothing wrong with using our abilities to process facts and come to conclusions or decisions, but our thoughts do not end there. Our minds continue to churn thought after thought about things that have already happened and the things that are yet to occur, and we get trapped in this vicious cycle.

So, when we engage in ceaseless thinking, we very easily lose touch with reality. We start living in our heads and fail to take action that can help us move forward in life. We often find ourselves fixating on things, constantly worrying and stressing over them, which ultimately drains our energy and motivation.

But what are the inner mechanics of fear that makes it such a prevalent challenge in modern times? Let's explore:

1. **Fear Is Not in the Present**

   Upon closer observation, we will find that we are consistently oscillating between the past and the future. We often reminisce about pleasant experiences from the past, only to immediately fret about whether they will never happen again. Similarly, when contemplating the future, our minds are inundated with all the potential mishaps and pitfalls that could occur. So, whether dwelling on past joys or future hopes, our minds habitually generate worries—either about reliving past hardships or the uncertainty of what lies ahead. As Jiddu Krishnamurti says, how fear arises, it is a movement of thought, time. When you are confronted with something immediately, there is no fear. It is only when thought comes in that there is fear.

Go back to a time when you were fully present and experiencing something, like a captivating sunset or an adrenaline-packed adventure. Chances are while you were fully present in that moment, there were no thoughts. Once the moment is over, the thoughts seep in. Depending on whether we loved it or hated it, our thoughts begin to stream in on wanting to experience it again or never again. Our thoughts move from one thing to the next, oscillating between the past and future, and trigger fear. Fear of unpleasant things happening again. Fear that the pleasant experiences and desires will never come true. In both these instances, we are never present. Thus, it is crucial to recognise a fearful thought is never rooted in the present. It is a movement of thought and time.

2. Desire Is the Root Cause of Fear

Fear, at its core, stems from a web of desires—desires for certain things to happen or not happen. These desires often arise from our attachments to certain events, people, or expectations. However, as adults, we have also had sufficient life experience to realise how much of it is beyond our control, and so we start to feel insecure.

In response to this insecurity, we are left to choose one of two paths. Some of us try to be in control of every little thing and plan obsessively to mitigate any possible hiccups that would affect our imaginary well-laid plans but feel shattered when after all these attempts, things still do not go our way. On the other hand, some of us get caught up in our heads and become paralysed in the process, leading to inaction and stagnation.

Eckhart Tolle emphasises, 'Not to be able to stop thinking is a dreadful affliction, but we don't realise this because almost everybody is suffering from it, so it's considered normal. This incessant mental noise prevents you from finding that realm of inner stillness that is inseparable from being. It also creates a false mind-made self that casts a shadow of fear and suffering.'

Fearless Living: Breaking Free from Limitations

We have normalised thinking 24x7 because everybody around us does it and suffers from it equally. But the endless chatter in our minds is making us sick from within. We torment ourselves with our fearful thoughts by letting our imaginations go wild and remain crippled under the weight of fear.

The only way we can liberate ourselves from the self-imposed shackles and unlock our potential is by detaching from the noise of our thoughts and realising there is no truth to the fear in our minds. This will allow us to be in the present moment without worrying about what was or what will be.

The entire yoga sutras compiled by sage Patanjali is an instructive manual on how we can bring to cessation the continuous modifications and emotional disturbances in our minds. *Yamas* (codes to transcend the world), *Niyamas* (codes to transcend yourself), *Asanas* (means to transcend the body), *Pranayama* (means to transcend the breath), and *Dhyana* (meditation) are five of the eight components (Ashtanga yoga) that help calm the mind and not get affected by the onslaught of thoughts. These practices combined with introspection, reflection, and contemplation are great ways to minimise thoughts, improve their quality, and gradually quieten the unnecessary chatter. And once we become more adept at managing our thoughts, the mind wanders less to the past or the future. With consistent practice, our perception is transformed, allowing us to live authentically and achieve our full potential.

Points to Ponder

Fear comes from desires that take us away from the present moment. Explore what's the source of your fear? What could open up for you in life if you stop your fears from calling the shots?

6
You Are Fine, Just Escaping Life

We are always looking for means to break the monotony of life. Whether it is through frequent travels to faraway shores, virtual escapades into OTT or social media black holes, or even indulging in substances, we need something to feel alive and keep going. In fact, there are a million other things that serve the sole purpose of distracting us from our boring and tiresome lives. But beneath their seemingly innocent façade, these escape mechanisms conceal an insidious core. Let's explore.

When we are just 'fine,' we can easily pass ourselves as thriving individuals, living our best lives. We are reasonably good at what we do and have tasted some bit of success but need respite every now and then to keep running the rat race.

During a particular phase of my life, I too found myself needing to constantly escape, and travel became my drug of choice. At the drop of a hat, I would book a trip and escape to faraway lands, where I was not shackled by my own self-imposed limitations. I would get lost in a new country and would roam carefree amongst unfamiliar people and surroundings. This was the only time I was 'me,' away from everything familiar. However, these moments of freedom were fleeting. My heart felt constricted, my smiles faded, as I returned to the routine of being 'fine' at my day job. Outwardly, I appeared to thrive, but inwardly, I began counting down to my next escapade.

The crucial point to understand here is that each of us may have a different method of escapism; it could be retail therapy, K-Drama, gaming, alcohol, luxurious spa massages, hosting events, or being a social media influencer. But they all serve the same objective of keeping us away from facing reality . . . a reality which is not going according to our hopes and expectations. And if we dig deeper, we will find that we are not ready to confront what our life has become, so we find ways to lull the soul into believing we are living empowered lives, which affords us the freedom and luxury of escape, to experience the world and its comforts. So, we continue enduring the unsatisfactory lives we find ourselves leading.

A dialogue from the movie *Karwaan,* where the late actor Irrfan Khan addressed a few carousing youngsters at a wedding party, is pertinent here: '*zara sa khush rehne ke liye itna nasha karna padta hai.*' It loosely translates to 'For a few drops of happiness, how much intoxication do people need.' Sounds familiar, doesn't it? This is the truth of our generation. We are so out of sync with reality that to feel anything, we need loud music, drugs, and escapades. Our lives don't fuel us adequately enough and don't challenge us to stretch our comfort zones. One could even say that our lives aren't truly suited for us, and instead of making meaningful changes, we simply go with the flow, inadvertently abusing everything around us because we lack a deeper understanding of what we truly need.

Japanese author, Haruki Murakami, wisely remarked: 'Closing your eyes isn't going to change anything. Nothing is going to disappear just because you can't see what's going on. In fact, things will even be worse the next time you open your eyes. That's the kind of world we live in . . . Closing your eyes and plugging up your ears won't make time stand still.'

The truth is that at some point, we must face reality. We need to confront our worst enemy, look it in the eye, and discover what's not working for us. Escaping is not the route. When we stop running away at the first glimpse of truth, when we dare to call a spade a spade and make amends to fix our lives for real, only then we will be truly fine. Travel, substances, and social media, all can be experienced and cherished in moderation. But in life, if we cannot function without them, we have a serious problem. Coming to terms with this reality is going to be hard initially. It will take time, but acceptance is the first step in this direction. Accepting that something about our seemingly successful lives isn't fulfilling is the initial stride toward discovering what truly will. It marks a fresh beginning where we embrace our reality, experiencing life as it is, without sugar-coating it to make it palatable. It will be bitter at first, but the sweetness will follow eventually if we stay on the path.

Remember, the only way to transform ourselves and start living fully is through embracing life and not running away from life. We are truly fine only when we muster the courage to face reality and accept 'what is' and not 'what ought to be.'

Points to Ponder

We can't escape the reality of our lives forever. Explore what's your go-to escape hatch? What does it absolve you from facing in your daily life? How can you learn to sit with what's not working in your favour currently?

7

YOU ARE FINE, BUT DISENGAGED

Does it feel like you are sleepwalking through life? That you are physically present but mentally checked out. That your work lacks fulfilment. That your relationships feel distant, as if an invisible barrier stands between you and your loved ones, hindering that sacred connection. Even the simplest tasks—eating, talking, working, sleeping, etc.—feel treacherous and mundane.

If you find yourself resonating with any of the points mentioned above, it is a strong indicator that you have become disengaged with life. So much so that nothing gives us that sense of fulfilment.

But what does being disengaged mean? In the simplest of terms, it means that our hearts are not fully invested. We cannot bring ourselves to do anything with our full commitment and vigour. This is not a capability issue, but a connection issue. There is a missing connection between what we truly desire and our reality, and our being gets warped due to this mismatch.

Say you were considering a job offer from a company and are told the many amazing things about the workplace, culture, and people. You are thrilled to hear all this and with high expectations accept the job offer. You join the company with much enthusiasm and hope but within a few weeks realise that not everything is as rosy as you had imagined. What happens next? You slowly withdraw yourself from the role, team, and company. That's exactly what happens to most adults.

As children, we were super-psyched about life, continually curious and in awe of everything in the world. As we grow up, we are fed narratives about what life will be and should be. Study well, get a well-paying job, and you are settled for life. Find your soulmate and eternal happiness will follow. Find your passion and you will never work a day in your life. We end up believing in the fairy tale of the happily ever after which we have been sold throughout our lives, only to get disappointed as adults when reality fails to live up to our expectations.

Eventually, we reach a mistaken conclusion that this is how the rest of our lives are going to be and lose ourselves in the process. We withdraw into a cocoon and start living superficially to protect ourselves from getting hurt any further. We move around and do things as required of us, but that's it. We do no more, no less, and derive no sense of accomplishment or fulfilment in the process.

Why We Disengage

The reasons why we might disengage from our work, relationships, and life at large are many. For some, it could be self-preservation because we feel we are not strong enough to endure the demands of reality. For others, it may arise from a lack of interest characterised by the classic 'what's in it for me to keep doing more of this' syndrome. Let's look at each of these facets in detail.

1. **Need for Self-Preservation**

   One of the primary reasons we withdraw and retreat into a self-created cocoon is self-preservation with the aim of shielding ourselves from the pressures and demands of the worlds and people around us. Either we are afraid of the situation or people around us, or we feel stuck and don't know how to extricate ourselves from our current life circumstances. So, we try to play it safe with the simple desire to protect ourselves from getting hurt at all costs. However, there are severe consequences for our emotional well-being and mental health when we isolate ourselves for extended periods. Over time, we inevitably lose our self-esteem and confidence.

2. **Lack of Intellectual Stimulation**

   Another common reason we disengage is because we are not interested in our daily activities. When the things we engage in day in and day out hold no interest to us or don't challenge us cognitively, it is natural to disengage. We see no point pursuing what we are doing because there's nothing in it for us. We just go through the motions, which only leads to a substandard output quality and a waste of time. As a result, the dwindling satisfaction leaves us with little motivation to get back to the task at hand, perpetuating a vicious cycle. Eventually, the dissatisfaction in one aspect of our lives spreads to other parts and weakens our spirit and overall self-worth.

3. **A Need for Purpose**

   Last, but definitely not least, disengagement in life can be brought about by the lack of meaning or purpose fuelling our lives. Mark Twain said, 'There are two important days in our lives. One when we are born and the second when we figure out why.' This lack of clarity about our purpose can leave us feeling adrift, as if we are navigating a ship without a compass. Without a clear sense of purpose, it is easy to feel lost and disconnected from our actions and surroundings. Moreover, this is the most prominent cause that leads people to become disengaged and disconnected in life. In the following section, we will explore strategies to overcome this challenge.

Finding Meaning in Life

In today's world, the pursuit of meaning and fulfilment often takes a backseat. The modern societal landscape tends to undervalue these aspects, leaving us complacent about seeking our true purpose. Moreover, the relentless pace and competitiveness of contemporary life leave us with scant time and opportunity to explore our authentic selves and identify what truly brings us meaning and fulfilment. So, we continue this pretence of being 'fine' without this meaning or purpose being our North Star and guiding our lives. This, in turn, leads us further away from our true selves.

The antidote to this form of disengagement is finding a connection with something bigger than us. This could be a connection with a community, a spiritual connection with our higher selves, or a connection with a cause driven by humanistic values. This connection helps channel our energies and unlock our unique sense of self. This also motivates us to continue striving towards something bigger and mightier than us.

To discover this connection, we need to stop settling for things in our lives that aren't so bad. When we settle for a partner who isn't as bad as others or a job that isn't as toxic as some others, we shut down a part of us that wants us to strive for more. When we venture beyond the surface to seek connections that fully engage us and compel us to extend our comfort zones, disengagement becomes impossible. By committing our entire being to the present moment, we leave no space for any aspect of ourselves to remain disconnected.

It is also essential to recognise that we are all unique individuals, shaped by our distinct experiences and interpretations. These experiences influence how we perceive the world, think, feel, and act. Consequently, our sense of meaning and purpose is also unique, stemming from our individual identities. Therefore, instead of trying to replicate someone else's calling, we must endeavour to discover our own purpose, aligned with our authentic selves.

Points to Ponder

Where in your life are you disengaging and why? What is within your control that you can act upon to feel more connected in that aspect of your life? How can you find that larger-than-life connection to something to propel you forward?

8

You Are Fine, but a Bystander

Some of us move through life unconsciously, tumbling and flailing at every turn. We are high in the skies when circumstances are favourable and down in the dumps when life doesn't go our way. We believe we have no control over how life pans out and give in to circumstances. Simply put, we go through life with a sense of resignation and helplessness. When we resign ourselves to our fate, we become mere bystanders, watching life pass us by. We believe life happens to us and that we are victims of our circumstances. We play no active role in shaping life according to our desires. Instead, we stand on the sidelines, watching from afar, and hope for success without actively participating in the journey. This passive approach leads to feelings of loneliness, dejection, and cynicism, which ultimately result in disappointment, frustration, anger, and rejection.

An important thing to note here is that when we feel like a bystander in life, it implies that we have an external locus of control. Locus of control, a concept developed by Julian Rotter in the 1950s, refers to an individual's perception of the underlying cause of events in their life. People with an internal locus of control believe they have control over the events and outcomes in their lives, whereas those with an external locus of control believe that events happen to them, without their influence. The underlying belief in the latter case here is that everything is predestined, and as a result, individuals may feel there's no need to do anything because events are perceived as beyond their control.

The Bystander Effect, a term coined by psychologists John Darley and Bibb Latané during the 1960s, describes the tendency for individuals to be less likely to intervene or take action in an emergency when others are present. Similarly, when we believe that our lives are predestined by a higher power or any other force, we may adopt a bystander mentality in our own lives.

Another common rationale for individuals with bystander syndrome is attributing their life circumstances to karma. While it's true that karma, or the consequences of past actions, shapes our present-day reality, it doesn't imply that everything is predetermined and beyond our control. This is a misunderstanding of karma. The law of destiny acknowledges that the present is influenced by past actions, but the law of karma extends beyond destiny by recognizing the concept of *purushartha* or self-effort. Humans are endowed with free will to make choices and take actions in the present moment. And while we cannot change our past, our self-effort remains independent of our destiny. There is free will. This means that at any given moment, when we opt for different choices and embark on a new path, we hold the power to shape our future. Thus, it is important to understand that what we encounter in life is predetermined destiny, but our response to it is defined by purushartha or self-effort. Through our actions today, we can change the trajectory of our destiny in the future.

In conclusion, in order to be truly fine, we need to stop playing the victim cards and radically accept and own our present circumstances. When we take full responsibility for our choices and actions, we start to take ownership of our lives and our future. We become an active player and not merely a bystander in our own lives. This doesn't mean that life becomes effortlessly smooth, free of all obstacles. Instead, it suggests that we develop the ability to navigate through life's ups and downs with greater ease and grace.

Points to Ponder

Shift the locus of control internally and take full responsibility for who you are and where you are today. Explore what actions can you take to be an active co-creator, not a bystander, in your life?

9
You Are Fine, but Emotionally Illiterate

Many of us often claim to be 'fine' when, in reality, we are nothing short of walking-talking volcanoes, teetering on the brink of eruption. With just a slight provocation, we unleash a torrent of emotions, unable to contain them. Similar to the words of the Joker in the movie *Dark Knight,* who remarked, 'Madness is like gravity . . . All it takes is a little push,' we find ourselves freefalling into a state of emotional chaos and imbalance with the gentlest of nudges. But why is it that even the smallest trigger can lead to a profound upheaval in our lives, and why do we often struggle to manage our emotions effectively? To understand this better, we will have to explore the makings and workings of emotions.

Emotions are nothing but energy in motion. Each thought, interaction, and task we encounter generates a specific emotional response, shaped by our past experiences and the interpretations we assign to them. Additionally, our understanding and handling of emotions often stem from the behaviours and attitudes modelled by adults during our formative years.

Some of us are taught to view emotions as a sign of weakness, leading us to suppress or dismiss them as insignificant. Others may never learn healthy coping mechanisms, resulting in a tendency to ignore or bury their emotions deep within. Such individuals often subdue their emotions and display little to nothing of what they really feel. They keep a tight rein on their words and actions and refrain from expressing what they feel. This doesn't mean that they don't have emotions; rather, they just curb the impulse to express what they feel.

Let's look at some of the prominent emotional archetypes in our modern-day society.

1. **The Ignorant**

   These individuals are emotionally illiterate, having spent years ignoring their emotions. Furthermore, they fail to recognise the imbalance in their feelings and merely go through the motions of life without ever lifting the veil to explore themselves.

2. **The Delusional**

   Individuals in this category often sense that something is amiss, yet instead of taking the time to identify or process their emotions, they deny their existence. This unconscious self-deception serves as a coping mechanism, providing them with the strength to carry on despite the underlying turmoil.

3. **The Escapists**

   Individuals in this category are inherently restless, often sensing and feeling a multitude of emotions but opting to distract themselves. They keep themselves busy with work, hobbies, or various distractions in order to avoid introspection into difficult emotions. As a result, they face compounded pain from the burden of unprocessed emotions along with the guilt or shame of their inability to confront them directly.

4. **The Victims**

   Individuals in this category often indulge in self-pity, adopting a victim mentality with thoughts like 'Oh, poor me!', 'Why me?', and 'Everything like this only happens to me'. Instead of actively seeking solutions, they tend to blame external factors for their difficulties, resulting in a stagnant state of being and helplessness.

5. **The Lone Wolves**

   Individuals in this category, often termed 'lone wolves,' struggle to process emotions and typically prefer to handle them independently. They tend to keep their feelings hidden and may appear stoic to those around them. Reluctant to seek assistance, lone wolves carry their emotional burdens alone, which can ultimately overwhelm them.

Emotions Influence Quality of Life

Emotions are not just arbitrary concepts; they have tangible effects on our bodies and translate into chemical imbalances within our bodies. For example, the heaviness we feel in our chest when we are sad or the butterflies in the stomach when we are anxious or nervous are not illusions but physical manifestations of our emotions.

In addition to its physical effects, emotional flux can profoundly affect our mental health. When emotions go unprocessed, our cognitive abilities suffer. Consequently, emotional imbalance can cloud our judgment and hinder our decision-making abilities.

Emotional turmoil can make us feel isolated, as if we are stranded on an island of our emotions. We may feel disconnected from the people around us, causing us to withhold our true thoughts and feelings. As Daniel Goleman, the father of Emotional Intelligence, suggests: 'If your emotional abilities aren't in hand, if you don't have self-awareness, if you are not able to manage your distressing emotions, if you can't have empathy and have effective relationships, then no matter how smart you are, you are not going to get very far.'

Therefore, to reach our fullest potential and lead fulfilling lives, nurturing our emotional intelligence quotient is just as crucial as developing our intellectual quotient.

Mastering Your Emotions: A 5-Step Guide

Here's a five-step guide to understanding and navigating the range of emotions we experience on a daily basis.

1. **Pause**

   First, we must pause long enough to feel what we are feeling instead of running to the next thing or escaping the emotions.

2. **Acknowledge**

   We may or may not be ready to process the emotion, but we must acknowledge it immediately. We can choose to resolve it at a later time after acknowledging the presence of the feelings.

3. **Identify**

   To effectively acknowledge what we feel, we need to identify the right feeling. In the beginning, look at emotion wheels online to appreciate the nuances of emotions we are capable of feeling and find out what most resonates with you at a given moment. Gradually as we stay more in touch with our feelings, we will be able to identify them faster.

4. **Infer**

   Take time to look back at the events that led to experiencing the emotions identified. Draw patterns and recognise people, conversations, and situations that arouse certain emotions. Is too much social media scrolling leading to more feelings of jealousy and inadequacy? Is being around certain people producing fear and making it harder to stand up for yourself? Then question the inferences. Is it true? Is it really true? Is there anything within your control to avoid experiencing unpleasant emotions? If you are dealing with heavier emotions, it might be good at this stage to ask for help from a clinical psychologist or coach.

5. **Act**

   Self-knowledge is pointless if you don't take action in a way that improves your quality of life. Take steps to pre-empt situations that cause unpleasant emotions, see what is in your control to be better prepared for them, and catch them before they ruin your day or week. Develop tactics to shift out of unpleasant emotions the moment you notice them.

All in all, with continuous and conscious effort, you will become better at addressing and navigating your feelings.

Points to Ponder

Which emotional archetype are you? How can you process your feelings better to experience emotional stability through your interactions and encounters?

10

You Are Fine, but a Workaholic

Many of us proudly wear the badge of being a workaholic. We are consumed by work, it permeates every aspect of our existence. The lines between work and life blur, merging our identity with our professional endeavours. Work becomes more than just a task; it becomes intertwined with our sense of self. The validation we seek from our work becomes deeply personal, driving an insatiable hunger for more. Our work is not just something we do; it begins to dictate who we are. Moreover, in the wake of the pandemic, the line between personal and professional life has further dissolved. Psychological detachment from work has become nearly impossible as it permeates every aspect of our lives through our devices and occupies our minds.

However, it's important to note that this phenomenon is not unique to the present day. Psychologist Wayne Oats coined the word 'workaholism' in 1971, defining it as 'a compulsion and uncontrollable need to work incessantly'.

There are a few takeaways from this definition. Firstly, our work has become a compulsion. Meaning, that when our attachment to work becomes excessive, our actions become compulsive. We feel the need to keep working, often inventing new tasks, handling duties that could be delegated, or redoing completed work in pursuit of perfection. The specific tasks are less important than the compulsion to keep busy, ensuring constant engagement.

Secondly, our work has become incessant. Meaning, we are constantly pulling all-nighters to finish a project, hoping that we then would return to a balanced routine afterwards, but this pattern keeps recurring. The fact is that we deceive ourselves, believing that once a particular milestone is achieved—finishing a project, securing a raise, or getting a company listed—things will ease up. Yet, this relentlessness cycle keeps going on until something eventually breaks down.

The Toll of Workaholism

Workaholism is often misunderstood as simply working long hours, but its true impact extends beyond the office. In today's world, workaholism is more about the inability to disconnect after work. It's about constantly ruminating about work, compulsively checking emails and messages, and feeling the need to follow up on tasks even outside of office hours. This pattern of behaviour, driven by an obsession with work, can significantly disrupt our work-life balance and overall well-being. Let's examine the impact of workaholism on our lives.

When we keep working compulsively and incessantly, the first aspect of our lives that suffers is our sleep routine. Being constantly burdened by work-related demands and pressures makes falling asleep difficult. Our minds remain active, running through a mental to-do list of pending tasks which makes it difficult to sleep. Over time, this lack of quality sleep deprives our bodies of the rest needed to recover and rejuvenate. Consequently, we wake up feeling even more exhausted, further increasing stress levels in the system.

Stress and anxiety inevitably follow, taking a toll on our physical well-being. This perpetual stress impacts our cardiovascular system, which has sadly become the norm in today's world. Moreover, high blood pressure and rising cortisol levels only exacerbate the issue. Operating under constant stress significantly increases our vulnerability to cardiovascular diseases, diabetes, and various other health complications.

Continuing to prioritise work over everything else also erodes our mental well-being. The constant grind leaves us mentally fatigued, impairing our ability to think clearly and make sound decisions. Moreover, our social life suffers as we withdraw from friends and family, resulting in feelings of isolation and disconnection. Constantly being in work mode drains us of both energy and the desire to engage in meaningful activities outside of work. We lack the motivation and vigour to pursue recreational activities that could help us unwind. Even if we have the time and energy, there's often little inclination to explore new interests or hobbies because we feel drained and depleted.

So, we can see how workaholism can have a pervasive and detrimental impact on all aspects of our lives.

Understanding Workaholism: Causes and Solutions

There are many reasons why we might become workaholics. The first and foremost is that it runs in the family. If we have been raised by parents who are sincere towards work, it is natural for us to equate success and positive attributes with incessant work. We start believing that working all the time is a sign of commitment and dedication, which shapes our relationship with our work.

Another significant reason for becoming workaholic is ambition. A desire for wealth and status can lead us to prioritise work over other aspects of our lives, as work can directly deliver the things we seek. But then our list of desires is endless, and thus, we remain workaholics throughout our adult lives. As soon as we reach a certain status, we start desiring more, perpetuating the cycle of work addiction.

Another reason for widespread workaholism is its role as a diversion. Work serves as a refuge, diverting our attention from the dissatisfaction or lack of fulfilment we may experience in other areas of our lives. By immersing ourselves in work, we sidestep the need to confront these issues directly. Additionally, the validation and recognition we receive in our professional roles may be lacking in other aspects of our lives, driving us to seek more of it through work.

All work and no play make Jack a dull boy and it applies to all of us as well. Too much of anything is not good and the same is the case with workaholism.

To achieve genuine well-being, it is crucial to establish a healthy work-life balance. This means not only enjoying the work we do but also knowing when to switch off and engage in activities outside of work. Setting clear boundaries on when work stops and leisure begins is essential. Outside of work, we can pursue personal goals such as reading new books, learning languages, improving fitness, travelling, cooking, gardening, photography, or engaging in artistic endeavours—anything that ignites our passion. Investing time in nurturing relationships with friends, family, and our broader community is equally vital. These connections provide invaluable support and stability, offering joy and fulfilment beyond the transient nature of professional roles and titles. By anchoring our lives in meaningful relationships, we create a solid foundation for long-term well-being and resilience.

Points to Ponder

Work is what we do to contribute to the world meaningfully and the sooner we detach our identities from our jobs, the better. Honestly assess for yourself, how often do you disconnect from work. How are your work levels impacting your health, relationships, interactions, and recreation?

Part II
How to Be Fine

11
What Does It Mean to Be Fine?

To achieve anything in life, we must first be clear about the end destination and then choose the appropriate direction as well as the means to reach it. The path to overall transformation is no different. Thus, we need to first understand where we are headed, and what benefits heading there will get us, and then find our path to effortlessly move in that direction.

In this section, we will explore what 'being fine' truly means, the benefits it entails, the obstacles on the path, and strategies to overcome them to ultimately reach a state of genuine well-being and fulfilment.

Definition of Being Fine

Being genuinely fine begins with feeling comfortable in one's skin. We are not in constant conflict with ourselves and can find our ground through good and bad times. We are not consumed by the rights and wrongs of the past or anxious about what tomorrow brings. There is more acceptance of current circumstances and trust in our abilities to find our way forward. There is lightness in our being and an alertness that comes from not living in our heads and worrying about everything.

Being fine also implies being in sync, where the body, mind, and intellect are in perfect alignment. Equanimity in the body translates to good health, ease of movement; strong functioning of the organs, energy to cope with the demands of our schedules, and an overall balanced state of being. Equanimity in the mind refers to mental stability, where constant fluctuations are under control and insecurities, fears, anxieties, and stress do not overtake rationality. Equanimity in the intellect translates to sharpness in decision-making and the ability to clearly discern all situations and identify the way forward without hesitation, doubt, or fear. Simply put, when we are fine, the body, mind, and intellect operate at their optimum levels. Additionally, when we are genuinely fine, our energies become more focused. The harmony between work and life is a natural consequence. We can allocate both mental and emotional resources to be fully present for our loved ones and show up at our optimum best at work. In this state, there is no room for insecurity, competition, or fear; instead, there is ample space for unconditional love to flourish.

More importantly, when we are truly fine, we meet life with enthusiasm and excitement instead of dread and despair. We rediscover the childlike wonder and eagerly anticipate each new day, looking forward to the opportunities it brings. At night, we go to sleep with a deep sense of gratitude, knowing that we did the best we could. Moreover, external events have less sway over us, as we remain rooted in our inner strength. Rather than reacting impulsively, we respond with mindfulness. Our demeanour is characterised by stability, and we navigate life's ups and downs with greater ease.

Now that we know what it means to be genuinely fine and all its dimensions, let's embark on our journey toward attaining it authentically.

12
Nurturing Balance

One key reason why many of us struggle to feel truly fine is due to a lack of balance in our lives. We have been navigating through constant stress, anxiety, or fear, essentially operating in a perpetual state of fight, flight, or freeze. Just as we can't instantly switch gears from four to one without slowing down the vehicle, we also can't transition from survival mode overnight. Therefore, before embarking on the journey to become fine, it is essential to restore our calm and achieve a state of equilibrium across all facets of our lives. Just as a wheel rolls smoothly when all its parts are balanced and working in harmony, so too must we achieve balance in all aspects of our lives. This includes calming our nervous system, alleviating mental turmoil, and regaining balance to lay the groundwork for our pursuit of true contentment and growth.

The Four Pillars of Life

Our lives consist of four interconnected and interdependent aspects: physical, mental, intellectual, and spiritual. Achieving genuine well-being and leading a fulfilling life requires us to balance each of these aspects. In contemporary times, a prevalent issue is the imbalance across these aspects of our lives. Often, we prioritise one aspect while neglecting or stumbling through the others, leading to an overall lack of equilibrium. For instance, if we were brought up valuing physical fitness above all else, we might prioritise exercise to the detriment of our emotional or spiritual well-being. Similarly, those taught to suppress emotions may neglect their emotional health until it manifests physically. Likewise, an emphasis on intellectual pursuits can lead to neglecting physical and emotional needs.

Let's delve into each of the four aspects individually, examining them in detail. As you go through them, take a moment to self-assess and consider what areas might need balancing in your life at present.

1. **Physical**

   Our physical bodies serve as the primary vessel through which we experience life. The food we consume, the sunlight we absorb, and the exercise we engage in all contribute to the vitality of our physical well-being. Neglecting or overlooking this fundamental aspect of life can hinder our ability to fully engage with the world around us and limit our capacity to pursue our goals. Therefore, in order to become fine, we must prioritise and nurture our physical health. By taking proactive steps to care for our bodies, such as maintaining a balanced diet, regular exercise, and sufficient rest, we empower ourselves to thrive in all dimensions of our lives.

2. **Mental**

   As humans, we are not just physical beings but also thinking and feeling entities. Our minds serve as the command centre for our thoughts, emotions, and perceptions, influencing how we interpret and respond to the world around us. Neglecting our mental health can lead to a myriad of challenges, including stress, anxiety, and depression, which can significantly impact our quality of life. Therefore, to truly be fine, it is essential to prioritise our mental wellness. This entails cultivating healthy coping mechanisms, practising mindfulness and self-care, and seeking support when needed. By nurturing our mental well-being, we enhance our resilience, emotional intelligence, and ability to adapt to life's ups and downs, ultimately fostering a greater sense of fulfilment and balance.

3. **Intellectual**

   Intellectual well-being encompasses our ability to think critically, solve problems, and engage in continuous learning and growth. Activities like reading and learning stimulate the intellect and prevent it from declining with age. These activities enrich the intellect and help the brain develop new neural connections and keep it healthy. Neglecting this aspect of ourselves can limit our cognitive abilities and hinder our capacity to adapt to new situations and challenges. Therefore, nurturing our intellectual well-being through activities such as reading, learning new skills, and seeking knowledge broaden our perspective, enhances our decision-making abilities, and empowers us to lead more fulfilling lives.

4. **Spiritual**

   Spiritual well-being forms an integral part of our overall health and happiness. It involves finding meaning, purpose, and connection to something greater than ourselves. Spiritual practices such as meditation, prayer, or mindfulness enable us to cultivate inner peace and a sense of harmony with the universe. Neglecting our spiritual health can lead to feelings of emptiness, disconnection, and existential distress. Therefore, it is integral to nurture our spiritual well-being through regular spiritual practices and self-reflection to foster a deeper sense of fulfilment, contentment, and alignment with our true selves.

Koshas

As mentioned above, the four quotients discussed contribute to our experience of life, and any imbalance among them affects the others, diminishing our overall well-being. However, this holistic approach to life is not a new or innovative concept; it finds its roots in ancient wisdom. Centuries ago, the Taittiriya Upanishads outlined the concept of *panchakosas* or the five sheaths encompassing our being. These include the *Annamaya Kosha, Pranamaya Kosha, Manomaya Kosha, Vignyanamaya Kosha,* and *Anandamaya Kosha.* Let's explore these.

The Annamaya Kosha, also known as the food body, represents our physical form, constituting the most tangible aspect of our being. Next is the Pranamaya Kosha, representing the energy body and the flow of life force known as *prana*. Following this is the Manomaya Kosha, or the mental body, which encompasses our thoughts and emotions and is subtler than the first two sheaths. Then comes the Vignanamaya Kosha, which pertains to the intellect and rational aspect within us. As we delve deeper, the sheaths become increasingly subtle, culminating in the Anandamaya Kosha, or bliss body, which defies clear definition.

According to the Upanishads, achieving harmony among the first four sheaths is essential to flourish as humans. When these layers are in equilibrium, the *Anandamaya Kosha* is dominant, resulting in a state of blissfulness. In this state, our life energies align, leading to feelings of equanimity, peace, joy, and profound bliss.

Finding Balance in All Dimensions

To embark on the path to genuine well-being, it's crucial to achieve balance across all dimensions we have explored. If you find your physical aspect lacking, prioritise rejuvenating your body. The fundamentals of diet, exercise, and sleep are widely known, yet often neglected in our technology-driven world, where sedentary work is the norm. Recognise the importance of movement; our bodies aren't designed for prolonged sitting. Strive to meet daily movement goals, aiming for 10,000 steps if feasible. If not, seek alternative ways to integrate physical activity into your routine, tailored to suit your lifestyle and commitments. One of my favourite methods involves combining physical movement with a dose of nature. There's nothing quite like walking amidst greenery or water bodies if such environments are accessible to you.

The act of moving settles the restless energies within our bodies, while nature has a calming effect on the mind, easing tensions and worries.

In today's fast-paced world, maintaining equilibrium in our mental quotient presents a significant challenge. Our minds are incessantly bombarded with chatter, thoughts, and emotions, often pulling us away from the present moment. Practices such as journalling and meditation offer effective tools for untangling this mental web. Journalling helps to clarify our thoughts, while meditation provides a space to process the multitude of emotions we carry within us each day. If the weight of our thoughts and emotions becomes overwhelming, it is crucial to seek professional support. Instead of battling our minds alone, therapists and psychologists can help us unravel the root causes of our mental turmoil and address them effectively.

If we find ourselves lacking intellectual stimulation, a great starting point is to embark on a journey of learning something new. This could be within our areas of interest but also challenging enough to push us beyond our comfort zones. Adopting a beginner's mindset, we open ourselves up to acquiring new knowledge and skills, fostering flexibility and openness to new ideas and experiences. Whether it is picking up a new language, learning to play a musical instrument, upskilling in our professional domains, or exploring a new hobby, the act of continual learning enriches our intellect and enhances our problem-solving abilities across various aspects of our lives.

The spiritual quotient, though the most subtle aspect of our lives, holds profound significance. Without a spiritual connection, no amount of health, mental peace, wealth, fame, or success can truly fulfil us. Recognising our deep interconnectedness with all beings and life itself, both on this planet and beyond, is essential for inner fulfilment. Without this recognition and spiritual growth, we may carry a sense of emptiness regardless of our external achievements.

Spirituality is a deeply personal journey and can take various forms for different individuals. It might involve religious practices, such as prayer or scripture reading, or simply embracing the oneness of all living beings. Whatever form it takes, it's important to carve out time and space for spiritual practices in our lives. For those unsure of where to begin, practices like *pranayama* or breathwork, which uses the breath to connect with higher energies, can serve as a starting point.

Engage wholeheartedly in your chosen spiritual practice, allowing yourself to be immersed in it with dedication and devotion. The transformative power of grace, although subtle, can profoundly impact our lives in ways beyond words can articulate. Strengthening our spiritual quotient can, in fact, serve as the cornerstone for balancing all other aspects of our lives. By consciously attending to each quotient, we transition from living on autopilot to living intentionally.

Points to Ponder

Rate your current lifestyle on a scale of 1-5 across these four quotients,1 being totally absent to 5 being fully aligned. Explore what practices you can inculcate in your daily routine to boost the quotients where its rating is currently below 3.

13

From Autopilot to Intentional Living

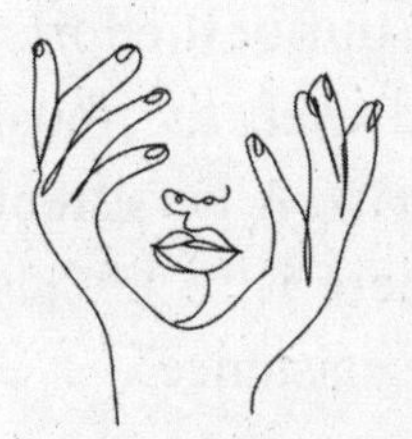

Now that we have covered the importance of attaining balance in all facets of life, it's time to get clarity on our definition of what constitutes a good life before we begin constructing it. This clarity is paramount because each of us possesses unique value systems, desires, and motivations. And unless we understand ourselves, we cannot build the good life we desire. Gaining this self-knowledge helps us understand what matters the most and prioritise it as we navigate through life.

Autopilot Living

Our modern lifestyles keep us in a state of running. From school to college to work, we find ourselves continuously moving forward without pausing to assess the direction of our journey. This frenetic pace leaves little room for contemplation or introspection, leading us to overlook the true potential of our existence. As we relentlessly pursue our daily tasks, we may eventually find ourselves caught in a monotonous routine that fails to fulfil us. Despite this realisation, many of us persist in repeating the same patterns day after day, further exacerbating the imbalance in our lives. This vicious cycle can leave us feeling trapped and disillusioned, longing for a sense of purpose and fulfilment that seems increasingly elusive.

For many of us, by the time the realisation hits, there are mounting responsibilities and commitments of being an adult: families to support, mortgages to pay off, and a lifestyle to uphold. All of these lead us straight into the open arms of an unwelcome companion: depression. Despite our best efforts, life seems to lose its flavour, joy dims, and even the most pleasurable experiences fail to ignite our spirits. A persistent question lingers in our minds: is this all there is to life? Is there something more beyond this mundane existence?

Breaking the Chain

The only way we can live our best lives is to break free from the shackles of autopilot living and start intentionally choosing what we want. When we live intentionally by checking in with ourselves about what we truly need, we can start to rebuild our life deliberately; a life where our gifts have a means to thrive, a life where we pursue what's most meaningful for us, a life where we actively participate as a co-creators and not passive victims.

Living intentionally necessitates self-awareness, a quality that prompts us to assess our present circumstances and confront a pivotal question often overlooked: What do we truly want in life? Without this self-awareness, we risk perpetually running on the hamster wheel of routine, never pausing to discover our individual answers to this essential question. In the upcoming chapter, we will explore strategies for cultivating awareness and attaining clarity about who we are and what do we genuinely desire in life, paving the way for us to live our most fulfilling lives.

14

Cultivating Awareness

To truly reconnect with our essence, the key ingredient we require is self-awareness. This invaluable quality enables us to turn inward and introspect to know what we really want in life. By cultivating self-awareness, we gain insights into our values, motivations, and purpose, guiding us towards a more authentic and fulfilling life. It empowers us to navigate challenges with clarity and make choices aligned with our true selves. But given the pivotal role self-awareness plays in our lives, why is it that so many people lack it in today's world?

The fact is that we are born with high levels of self-awareness but are then quickly educated about the ways of the world. In the process, we stow away the wisdom we are born with to make space for things deemed necessary for survival in this big bad world which often comes at the expense of our innate understanding. Consequently, many of us lack a genuine connection with ourselves and remain unaware of our true essence. Our identities become entwined with external factors such as our occupation, social status, possessions, and relationships, leaving little room for introspection or self-discovery. We don't know who we are beyond these external identities and if someone strips us of these titles, we would be lost.

Moreover, fundamental questions like what our true nature is, what we most value, what piques our interest, what makes our hearts sing, and what we are here for are not asked, explored, or encouraged. So, when someone specifically asks about our desires or aspirations, we find ourselves stumbling for answers. The first step to finding clarity is to reconnect with our true selves. While we may possess a superficial understanding of our identity, it merely scratches the surface of self-awareness. Beneath this veneer lies a complex tapestry of layers waiting to be unravelled.

Unconscious to Conscious

Objectively viewed, all we are is a concoction of facts, interpretations, perceptions, memories, stories, and some bit of pure fantasy. Although we often perceive ourselves as rational beings, many of the notions we hold about ourselves are narratives we have constructed rather than objective truths. These narratives typically reside in the subconscious rather than the conscious mind, shaping our perceptions and behaviours without our awareness. Despite their profound influence, these underlying beliefs often remain concealed from our conscious awareness, operating beneath the surface of our thoughts and actions.

So, to design the life of our dreams and be truly fine, we need to dig deep and decode these stories, perceptions, and inferences. We need to bring out all aspects of who we are from our subconscious state to consciousness. We need to bring forth the narratives that play non-stop in our subconscious mind and evaluate them in the light of truth, in the light of who we truly are and aspire to be.

Understanding ourselves is an ongoing journey, not a single task to be completed. The question of who we are is intricate and constantly evolving. It's a process that unfolds gradually, much like peeling away layers of an onion. To embark on this journey, we must first cultivate greater consciousness and awareness.

So, let's shed the weight of what we know, wear the hat of curiosity, and delve into some pressing existential questions to gain more self-knowledge. The following are some important questions that prompt introspection and soul-searching:

1. Who am I?
2. What do I value most?
3. What is my definition of success?
4. What does my ideal day look like?
5. What is most meaningful for me to engage with in this life?

When we become aware of our unique answers to these questions we lay the foundational blocks of intentional living. Instead of our default outside-in way of living, our desires emanate consciously from within and guide our actions. These intentional choices help us transcend our autopilot ways of being. This awareness also gives us the conviction to hold our ground and pursue our choices regardless of whether the world around us approves or validates them. When we live consciously, in line with our true nature, life starts to feel much more enriching and fulfilling. We let go of the endless chase for more and are left wanting for nothing. The elusive contentment and satisfaction we seek naturally emerge as a consequence of intentional living.

15
Discovering the Self

'Who am I?' is an existential question, that philosophers and the wise spend their entire lives exploring. But our purpose is not philosophising or debating this query. Instead, it's to understand ourselves sufficiently to design a life where we can truly thrive. The most effective approach to achieving this is to start by identifying what we are not. It is important to understand that we are not defined by our jobs, designations, economic status, social standing, material possessions, relationships, past accomplishments, children, parents, religion, nationality, community, experiences, mind, or body. As we shed what we are not, one layer at a time, we come closer to our true selves. Additionally, understanding what we are not also helps us detach from the many identities we associate with.

Who Are We Then?

As the popular saying goes, we are spiritual beings having a human experience and not the other way around. We are woven in the same fabric and essence as the magnificent creator and all of creation. We are the particle and the wave. We are transient and eternal, insignificant and omnipotent. We are everything and nothing. I could go on and on describing the unlimited nature of our being, but there's only so much language crafted by finite human minds can convey. The truth is that the depth and essence of who we are can only be understood through experience. It defies description.

The beauty of human life is that we come undefined. We are born as a seed of possibility that we can nurture and mould to fit any shape or size. Our contribution to the world can be as big or as small as we aspire.

So, once we shed all that we are not and experience the fullness of our being, we gain clarity about who we would like to be, the qualities we resonate with, and the values we would like to live by. And when we go beyond our temporary bodies and connect to the eternal self, we automatically drop our attachments to the transient identities and open up to unlimited possibilities.

The X-Factor

What truly sets humans apart, making our journey through life more consequential? Humans are not merely programmed automatons from birth. Instead, we are born as seeds brimming with untold possibilities.

Most animals and plants lead lives largely dictated by the instincts and patterns hardwired into them by nature. With more primitive intellects, they are far more susceptible to being governed by base impulses and instincts than highly conscious humans. A deer essentially has one set role to fulfil in its lifetime. So too does the tiger, the centipede, the bee, or the banyan tree. What they are is pre-decided at birth, and so is the narrow path of what they will become.

But human beings are not bound to such a straightforward, predetermined existence. A human life is one ripe with open-ended possibilities. We are born carrying the seed of our highest potential within us—a seed that can blossom into the full flowering of a generous, self-actualized being, or remain shrivelled as the seed of an unlived, unfulfilled life.

We are born for greatness, not with intrinsic greatness itself. We must put in the conscious effort to nurture and tend to that seed, to allow it to flourish into its highest expression. That means the ultimate shape of our lives is in our own hands. But for us to truly design lives of purpose and meaning, we must first awaken to the transformative power simmering within our core.

Let me share the story of the eagle and the chickens. There was once a mighty eagle that made its nest beside a towering mountain. One day, the eagle laid four eggs, but one egg accidentally rolled down the mountain and landed amidst a clutch of eggs in a chicken coop below. The eaglet hatched and grew up together alongside the brood of chicks, never knowing a different world existed. So, the eaglet joined its chick companions—clucking, cackling, scratching for worms, and thrashing its wings to feebly fly just a few feet off the ground.

Years passed by. The eagle grew old and weary, continuing to live out its days grounded to the earth just like every other chicken in that coop. But then one fine day, the aging eagle looked up and saw a magnificent bird gliding high up in the boundless blue skies. The eagle watched, transfixed, as this winged creature navigated the winds effortlessly, barely fluttering its outstretched wings as it soared amongst the clouds.

The eagle couldn't contain its wonder, turning to the chickens and asking what sort of creature that was. The chickens clucked their ready reply: 'Why, that is an eagle, the king of all birds. It belongs to the sky.'

Yet despite belonging to the sky more than the earth below, the eagle lived out the rest of its days confined to the chicken coop, pecking at the ground amongst its flightless feathered friends, ultimately dying as just another chicken and never realising its true identity or soaring potential.

This is the tragedy that most of us humans unconsciously live out as well. We are born one day, we grow up, we work, we die—never once discovering or embodying our authentic, spirited selves. We live our entire lives like cattle raised merely for slaughter, carrying the heavy burden of yet another unrealised, unlived life . . . generation after generation after generation.

Self-discovery Exercise

Once we clear out the cache of all that we are not, a good way to identify who we truly are is through analogies or metaphors. Let's look at an example.

Imagine yourself beyond the confines of human existence. If you could embody anything other than a person, what would it be? This choice represents your metaphor—a symbol that reflects your essence and aspirations. It might be a natural element, an animal, an object, or any entity you deeply resonate with. Ensure your metaphor is expansive, encompassing all facets of your being and your aspirations.

For instance, my metaphor is the ocean. Here's why:

On the surface, I am relentless like the waves, constantly learning, discovering, and pushing my boundaries. Beneath it all, I am calm and still like the depths of the ocean, as I don't attribute much value to any accomplishments in the external world. And like how every wave is different in its intensity, form, and speed, I believe all aspects of my life should be new and brimming with vitality. A life where every day feels like a new adventure.

The waves also symbolise impermanence, a concept that deeply resonates with me as I continuously grapple with the desire for both the fleeting and the eternal in my life. And just like a single drop doesn't make an ocean, I believe my life derives meaning from this collective power. This belief inspired the creation of 'Being Meraklis'.

There is also a shadow-side to our metaphors. Mine is that I am relentless in my pursuit, which leaves me drained. And just like the planetary alignment impacts the waves, I am affected by my mood swings. One moment, I am soaring high in the sky; the next, I am down in the dumps.

So, think about what your metaphor is; draw it out, write the adjectives that resonate with you, and visualise them. If feasible, take some time to meditate; this can help bring forth new insights and ideas. Remember, your metaphor may evolve over time as you grow and your circumstances change. Embrace this natural evolution process. Revisiting this exercise every few years can be a valuable tool for self-discovery and personal growth.

Define Success Your Way

As we deepen our understanding about ourselves, it's important to go further and define what success means to us. We have been conditioned to believe that wealth, fame, and glory are the only possible definitions of success, whereas success comes in various shapes and sizes, just as humans do.

The reason why our autopilot ways of living don't feel satisfying is that we are chasing conventional metrics of success without pausing to check if what we are chasing matches our definitions of success. To know our definition of success and keep track of it, with each passing day, we need to adopt techniques like journalling, which helps us stay tuned to ourselves, our needs, and our evolving desires.

Journalling: A Tool to Understand the Self

Writing a journal regularly reveals patterns about how we think, feel, and act. It is an effective technique to help disentangle thoughts and comprehend unexpressed desires. We understand what drives, triggers, energises, and inspires us. Journalling provides an invaluable space to dig deeper and uncover what truly motivates our behaviours and patterns from the inside out. It helps us examine and potentially tweak the inputs and processes driving how we move through life. It also allows us to dig deep beyond the superficial layers and borrowed personalities to tap into who we authentically are at our core, and what we most aspire to accomplish in this fleeting human journey. To find success that doesn't ultimately feel hollow and unsatisfying, we need to find those answers from the resonant depths of our own being—not merely scrape the surface layers.

The practiced art of journalling helps bring certain profound truths to light that often remain hidden from our conscious, day-to-day minds. There are particular self-realisations that we have unconsciously captured but which fail to surface until we create space and time to allow them to emerge. This is another powerful way that journalling facilitates self-discovery, as it gently reveals insights about ourselves that we innately need to see and integrate but haven't fully experienced yet.

The regular practice of thoughtful journalling quite literally creates the spaciousness for us to discover more about the authentic experiences unfolding within us, beneath the superficial exterior of merely coasting through and declaring ourselves 'fine.' It provides an outlet to freely express our unconscious desires and core callings, pointing us towards the paths and modes of being that could ultimately offer lasting fulfilment.

The Art of Journalling

If pen and paper doesn't appeal to your style, we live in a world of digital apps. You can maintain a digital journal or even an audio-based one. Pick whatever comfortable medium resonates, but the key is to start. The act of journalling itself is far more important than the specific format or fancy stationery.

You can journal each morning before the day begins. Capture how you authentically feel and set an intention for the upcoming day. This practice helps us remain more conscious and present throughout the hours ahead. Write out your plans and why those tasks hold importance, as well as the potential consequences of not following through. These reflections allow us to truly prioritise what matters most and not get lost in aimless firefighting or mindlessly living out the world's agenda for us.

For those who aren't morning people and tend to hit the ground running, there is another way journalling can be beneficially used—at the end of each day. It can become a reflective practice to thoughtfully capture the day's thoughts, emotions, experiences, and evaluations of our actions, one day at a time. You can develop a winding down routine to wrap up the workday by capturing how it truly unfolded—what went well, what didn't, what felt most challenging, and what you might want to do differently tomorrow. It is a simple technique that likely takes less than 5 minutes. But in the long run, it exponentially helps us achieve greater clarity and growth.

As the famous Roman philosopher Seneca wisely stated, 'Before the darkness falls, I go over what I have done during the day and take an old-fashioned inventory.' He recommended pondering questions like:

- What progress have I made today?
- In what ways have I actively been a good friend to myself?
- What bad habit did I counter or improve upon?
- Which faults or shortcomings did I take a stand against today?
- In what respects am I better than I was yesterday?

This ritual of self-reflection empowers us to make more conscious choices that positively shape the ongoing trajectory of our lives.

To summarise, it doesn't ultimately matter which specific technique is used, but try to cover intentions, affirmations, gratitude, and reflections in a daily journalling practice. Inculcating this cathartic habit of journalling every single day could very well connect us to our authentic deeper selves faster than any other technique. Additionally, beginning with a meditation practice before journalling can also help shed external influences and ingrained biases, allowing us to become truly honest with our real selves before putting pen to paper and discovering our true self.

Points to Ponder

Start by completing the sentence: 'I am someone who is . . .' and keep adding adjectives and qualities to it. Avoid defining yourself by your job or the external identities you hold. Review it periodically and modify it as you grow and evolve through life's many ups and downs. Deepen your self-knowledge and chase what gives you meaning and satisfaction.

16
Know Your Values

Another effective method for discovering our true selves is to identify our values—the ideologies we live by and aspire to embrace. Values serve as our fundamental guiding principles; they provide meaning, influence our actions, and drive our behaviour. When we remain faithful to our guiding principles, we make decisions and behave in ways that align with our authentic selves. Values enrich our lives with significance and assist us in determining what we aspire to experience.

Begin with Your Inspiration

To begin identifying values that resonate with you, take a moment to reflect on the individuals who have influenced you throughout your life. Consider those you admire, friends who inspire you to grow, and mentors whose guidance has shaped your journey. Make a list of these influential figures and then delve deeper into the qualities they embody that inspire you. Take notes on these qualities, whether it's kindness, perseverance, honesty, or any other trait that stands out to you.

Once you have identified these qualities, take another step forward and recall specific behaviours or actions of these individuals that have left a lasting impression on you. Reflect on how these behaviours align with the values you have identified and consider how they manifest in real-life situations. By observing and documenting these behaviours, you will gain a deeper understanding of how values translate into action and how they can shape your own behaviour and decisions.

Next, get specific and pick five values that resonate with you from the list given on page 120. It doesn't have to be 100 per cent precise. Choose the five that make the most sense at this stage of your life. These could be values you currently embody and those you aspire to adopt, depending on your goals and aspirations. When selecting values, be mindful to avoid choosing words with similar meanings. Opt for the term that resonates most deeply with you and truly represents how you envision yourself.

Prioritise Your Values

Once you have identified your top five values, rank them in order of importance. Assign the value that holds the utmost significance and is non-negotiable as number 1, followed by 2, 3, 4, and 5 accordingly. While the hierarchy may shift over time due to evolving life circumstances, having a prioritised order assists in navigating life's dilemmas and making decisions more efficiently.

For instance, suppose authenticity ranks highest for you, followed by creativity and community. Now, imagine receiving an intriguing collaboration opportunity—a project that promises creativity, challenge, and impact on your target audience. However, it entails conforming to certain norms that contradict your authentic self and beliefs, compromising your ability to act authentically.

Value Words		
Authenticity	Forgiveness	Love
Achievement	Freedom	Loyalty
Adventure	Fun	Openness
Balance	Grit	Optimism
Boldness	Growth	Partnership
Challenge	Happiness	Peace
Collaboration	Harmony	Playfulness
Community	Honesty	Presence
Compassion	Honour	Recognition
Connection	Humour	Respect
Courage	Independence	Responsibility
Creativity	Inner Peace	Simplicity
Curiosity	Innovation	Spontaneity
Determination	Integrity	Stability
Ease	Joy	Trust
Excellence	Justice	Vitality
Empathy	Kindness	Zest
Fairness	Learning	

Now, imagine if you hadn't prioritised your values. Faced with a collaboration offering creativity and community, it would be challenging to discern what aligns best with your true self. However, with the hierarchy clearly established, where authenticity is the most important value for you, the answer to this collaboration becomes a clear no.

Remember, our values serve as guiding principles that define what is most important to us and, consequently, contribute to shaping our identity with greater clarity.

Living Your Values

It's not enough to identify our core values. We need to translate them into actions in our daily lives to feel that sense of alignment. For every value in your top 5 list, write out what that value means to you. For example, if integrity is your top value, to you it might be being honest in your speech and actions. Or if freedom is your top value, it might mean liberty to choose what you would like to do and when. Depending on your core values, define them in a way that resonates with your belief systems.

Next, write down 2-3 ways in which that value manifests in your daily activities, interactions, and decisions. Continuing the example of holding integrity as a core value, you might list down its manifestations as:

- Being truthful in my interactions with others.
- Being honest in my work and transactions.
- Not indulging in gossip.
- Admitting when I make a mistake.

This helps in making abstract notions like values concrete.

Third, and probably most crucial, make sure to articulate ways that contradict your core values. These are thoughts or actions that make us feel like we are out of alignment with our value systems. If integrity is your core value, a few ways you could go out of alignment is by not keeping your word. When you commit to doing something for yourself or others and don't follow through, it could be a breach of integrity. Articulating this can help us be more mindful of such situations, reducing the chances of us going out of alignment in day-to-day life. What we value is a crucial aspect of how we experience life. We must make sure to live by our values. A good practice to live our values is to reflect at the end of the day on where we managed to live by our values and where we can do better. Such daily reflections help us make sure that we are leading lives aligned with our core value systems.

Points to Ponder

On a scale of 1-10, rate each value on how well your life and actions are aligned to it, 1 being nowhere close and 10 being aligned. Look at the values which you have rated lower than 5 and identify what actions you can take to be more aligned.

17
Build Confidence

After nurturing balance and gaining clarity, confidence is the next integral thing that we need in our journey to be truly fine. But what do we mean by self-confidence? In simple terms, it is the belief that we can rely on ourselves, achieve goals, and attain success. Believing means trust, conviction in abilities, courage to act despite fears; the sense to learn from mistakes and chase cherished dreams. It is living with the realisation that everything we need to know is within us, a belief that we have the power to create and fight for the life we desire. Sadly, that level of confidence is farfetched for most of us. The harsh truth is that as adults, we believe in everyone but ourselves. This lack of self-belief makes it harder to achieve goals and live on our own terms.

In this chapter, we delve into the roots of self-doubt and fear, debunk common misconceptions surrounding confidence, address the distinction between confidence and arrogance, and provide actionable strategies to cultivate greater confidence.

Reasons We Lack Confidence

There are many factors that can contribute to a low self-confidence, but two primary barriers that hinder our confidence are self-doubt and fear. Let's look at each of them in detail.

We all tell ourselves stories about who we are and why we are the way we are. These are stories that we have developed over the years. From early childhood, through every interaction, experience, success, failure, hurt, and loss, we have added dimensions and flavours to who we think we are. Over time, we sprinkle these stories with labels and analogies to ensure we file every experience the 'right' way, something which aligns with our interpretation of them.

By the time we are in our 20s, we have a solid narrative about who we are—I am shy, I am an introvert, I am not a public speaker, I am sensitive, I am a failure, I am unlucky, I am unlovable, etc. The more we set our labels in stone, the more we seek out similar experiences and gather more evidence to validate our beliefs and pre-conceived notions.

Whether we believe we are good or not, we are right. It's not the events, but our interpretations that define us. This is why children born and raised by the same parents in the same external contexts still grow up to be unique individuals with distinct identities, beliefs, and values. This nuance might make things a bit more complicated and simpler at the same time. Complicated because we need to spend time and energy detangling these interpretations and setting the records straight, and simpler because changing these stories is very much in our control. We can break out of these shackles by rewriting our stories.

We doubt ourselves extensively due to the excessive emphasis we have been conditioned to place on seeking external validation. Let's explore this in detail.

Since childhood, we have been told to place our trust outside of ourselves—schools, teachers, parents, priests, colleges, mentors, corporates, government—any institution or person outside of us. When these external institutions or people praise us, we take it as a positive sign. We place our trust in their trust. When they don't, our faith in ourselves sinks.

This is likely what happened with most of us. We had a dream, we worked on it, and put it out in the world and it wasn't as well received as we had hoped. Adults might have made fun, said it wasn't good enough, or told us we must stick to things we know better or praised someone else. The seed of doubt is sown, leading to questions like 'Am I good enough?', 'What if I am not cut out for this position?', and 'Do I deserve this?'

The important thing we need to understand here is that confidence that comes from external validation is on a shaky foundation. If our belief comes from others' belief in us, we will always be at their mercy. Our self-worth will plummet when kindness is not bestowed upon us. We need to realise that belief is not outside-in, it is inside-out. Others cannot ignite a spark that we are yet to light from within. We need to set the play in motion by believing in ourselves and having confidence in our abilities. When we trust our truth and operate from that deep sense of knowing, our belief becomes unshakeable. From this space of self-assurance, belief from others is a bonus but not a necessity.

The Impact of Not Believing in Ourselves

When we don't believe in ourselves, a lot of things go off balance. We don't prioritise what's right for us and allow people to encroach upon our personal boundaries and dictate what we must or mustn't do. We act from a place of low self-worth and self-doubt that leaves us feeling drained, demotivated, and miserable. We never pause to acknowledge our achievements, only keep harping about our faults. We don't ask for what is rightfully ours; not the promotions, not the salary hikes, not the space in our relationships, nothing.

Soon, we start avoiding situations and stop taking chances because we are too hard on ourselves. We start to settle for scraps, merely exist, and end up calling that a living. This would have worked if we are sleepwalking through life and remaining ignorant. But now that we know what our heart truly desires, what makes life most meaningful, there is no looking back. We need to overcome doubt, worry, and fear to live the life of our dreams. We need to get to the root of the lack of self-belief and address the issues. We need to identify the source of our self-doubt and reframe it into something more empowering.

Words of Wisdom

Indian scriptures offer another route to tackle doubting ourselves. In Bhagavad Gita, Lord Krishna tells Arjuna that we need to know the nature of our true selves. While humans perceive the world with their five senses, it is but an illusion and not a reality. Who we are beyond these impermanent bodies is true awareness, boundless energy that is one with the source of this universe—whether we would like to call it God or The Supreme Creator or Cosmic Force.

When we truly understand this, we realise there's nothing good or bad, no one superior or inferior, we just are. There's no space for crippling self-doubt or limiting beliefs once we realise this oneness we share with the cosmic power.

Connecting with the higher force allows us to overcome the self-limiting stories we tell about ourselves and go beyond doubt. This leads us to live a life without any limitations . . . a life we truly deserve.

Fear: An Enemy to Self-Confidence

Another major reason we lack self-confidence is fear. Fear can manifest in many insidious forms and guises and can grip us with a force like none other, holding us back from pursuing the things we genuinely want to achieve in life. Fear also compels us to stick to the well-trodden, familiar path that our mind knows and doesn't have to expend additional energy navigating. The biggest consequence of fear is paralysis of action. It stops us dead in our tracks from taking any real steps forward, and this inertia can manifest itself in different ways. For some, it breeds endless procrastination. We continually put things off until another day, rather than confronting our fears head-on by doing the difficult things today. For others, fear takes the form of perfectionism. We shovel all our anxieties under the rug and try to fool the world, and even ourselves, believing we are merely striving to get it perfectly right and simply aren't ready yet. For many, it emerges as an obsessive worry about potential exclusion, rejection, or judgment. We constantly wonder what others might think, say or snidely comment, paranoid about disappointing them. So, we remain hopelessly stuck in inaction.

What we need to understand is that failure actually teaches some of life's most vital lessons. Our most startling revelations and transformative growth often come precisely when we have hit rock bottom, when we cannot sink any lower and finally choose to change course. As children, we learnt to walk by stumbling and falling repeatedly. We didn't understand how to truly balance on a bicycle until we fell over and over again. Everything of real value that we have learnt, we have absorbed through taking imperfect action, making errors, unlearning, and then relearning the right way forward. Failure gives us the courage to fight with every last ounce of grit we possess, even when our back is against the wall and the path ahead seems impossible. Failure teaches humility, discretion, and wisdom in a way that success alone never could.

Thus, we need to face our fears head on and not avoid them. In the following section we will discuss how we can do so.

Ways to Overcome Fear

1. **Identify the Source of Fear**

   Analyse the specific thoughts connected with your fears, logically and objectively. I prefer asking myself how I would respond if a close friend confided that they were afraid of doing something for the same reasons. We are often far kinder and more compassionate towards others than we are to ourselves. When we review these fearful thoughts from an outside perspective, we may unravel hugely exaggerated versions of certain truths and get down to the root core of what we are actually afraid of.

   If what you are catastrophising over is merely hypothetical worry, consciously dismiss it and refuse to let your mind tumble down that rabbit hole. If the fear does seem legitimate upon inspection, analyse it as rationally as possible. What is this fear truly trying to alert you to? How factually accurate are the thoughts and stories associated with it? What are the realistic possible outcomes you are worried about? How many of those potential outcomes are truly unfavourable or terrible? What proactive steps could you take to minimise the chances of those worst-case scenarios occurring?

Through thorough and rational analysis, we will discover that many of our fears are unfounded and by breaking them down logically, we can uncover their true nature and understand them better. All in all, this process will empower us to confront fears with clarity and resilience.

2. Sit with Fear

Our first instinctive reaction when we feel gripped by fear is to try to escape that uncomfortable feeling. We distract ourselves, stay busy with other activities—anything that helps us avoid confronting the fear head-on. But the only way through to the other side is to commit to sitting with our fears, truly feeling into them and getting intimately acquainted.

So, the next time you find yourself holding back from taking a risk or chance because you are afraid of potential failure, don't reflexively run or numb out. Instead, try sitting still with the fears arising. Acknowledge and accept that the feeling of fear is presently there. Rather than unconsciously avoiding the discomfort, spend quality time exploring what this particular fear is trying to signal to you and where it may be originating from. Listen to the fear without judgment, feel into it, unpack it and then take wise action despite its presence.

The fears will likely remain, but you don't have to be controlled by them anymore. You can stare them down, embrace the uncertainty they represent, and decide to move forward anyways towards what you know is important and meaningful to you.

Confidence Is Not Arrogance

Most of us think being confident is equivalent to being arrogant, but these are two very different concepts. Let's look at the differences between the two.

Confidence is believing you can do what it takes, arrogance is believing you can do it better than everyone else. When we are arrogant, our ego takes centre stage, and there is an in-built sense of superiority. The ego prides itself on being better than others and not just being better. It's relative and forces us to surround ourselves with people worse off than us. But that's not confidence.

Confidence is mere self-belief that we know who we are and what we bring to the table in a conversation. It's objective and doesn't involve comparison but a simple awareness of our ability and competence. We can be confident, yet humble.

Here the term that author Adam Grant coined in his book is the perfect fit, 'Confident Humility.' He writes, 'Confident humility is knowing how little you know and how much you're capable of learning. It's being secure enough in your knowledge to recognise your ignorance—and secure enough in your strengths to acknowledge your weaknesses.'

Humility acknowledges the limitations of our knowing and opens up possibilities to learn and evolve continually. It keeps us grounded. While confidence in our abilities implies, we can pursue and achieve what we set our minds to. We need both to live intentionally.

Myths About Self-Confidence

Let's look at the three wrongly placed notions we have about self-confidence:

1. **We Are Not Born with It**

   Confidence is not something governed by genetics. It is a learned skill, not an innate trait. We are not born with confidence. Like any other skill, confidence needs to be proactively cultivated over time through deliberate practice. This means that regardless of where we currently stand on the confidence scale, we can work towards raising our levels. It also means that losing confidence is not the end; it simply takes focused effort and patience to rebuild it.

2. **Confidence Is Regardless of Context**

   Confidence levels are not uniform across all aspects of our lives. We might feel very confident in a professional setting but lack confidence when it comes to parenting. We are contextual beings, and our confidence levels also vary depending on the context. Or if we are doing something we have failed at before, like public speaking, our confidence plunges when we step up to the microphone, even if we are usually comfortable speaking to strangers one-on-one. The important point to note here is that everyone has areas of weakness, and that confidence is purely situational and contextual—it needs to be honed individually across each aspect of life to attain mastery.

3. **Confidence Doesn't Come First**

There is a common misconception that we need confidence first in order to find success. It's actually the other way around—success feeds and fuels higher levels of confidence. In *Confidence Competence Loop*, as described by American motivational speaker Mel Robbins, our initial attempts may result in either success or merely surviving the endeavour. However, through surviving, we glean valuable lessons and cultivate the courage to persist until we ultimately achieve success.

Thus, we can see that self-confidence stems from the decision to keep taking risks, to bet on ourselves to succeed, and to keep progressing through life's competency loop. In other words, confidence doesn't magically arrive first; it's the courage to accept failure while persistently trying that builds lasting confidence over time.

How to Build Confidence

Here are some ways to boost self-confidence as we overcome doubts, worries, and fears.

Firstly, start with imitation. If we have never truly felt confident in life, this might be the easiest entry point. Mimic someone you believe exudes confidence. How would they think, feel or act in a given situation? Until we find our own authentic sense of confidence, we can begin by emulating their behaviours. This can only be effective if we intimately know the person and have closely observed their mannerisms first-hand.

Secondly, simply begin somewhere. The biggest obstacle lack of self-confidence presents is that it prevents us from even trying in the first place. We procrastinate and avoid taking any action. But inaction only further lowers our self-esteem. So, identify small, manageable steps towards those bigger desired goals, and make sure to start putting one foot in front of the other. As the American statistician W. Edwards Deming said, 'Don't wait until everything is just right. It will never be perfect. There will always be challenges, obstacles and less-than-perfect conditions. So what? Get started now. With each step you take, you will grow stronger and stronger, more and more skilled, more and more self-confident, and more and more successful.'

Thirdly, be okay with imperfect action. Many times, we lose confidence because we are afraid that we won't be able to execute something perfectly right away. Remember how we learned to walk as children? How many times and ways did we fall before we could finally stand tall on our own two feet? So many endeavours in life are similar. Ask yourself, what's the worst that can happen if the action is imperfect or the results are disastrous? Even worst-case scenarios of most endeavours are reversible. When we can truly see that there's little, if not none, irreversible damage for most actions in life, we can allow ourselves to take imperfect, stumbling actions until we gain real mastery. Enhance your tolerance for the messy imperfections involved in any worthwhile pursuit.

The next time you stop yourself from doing something due to a lack of confidence, remind yourself of this simple truth: you try, you fail, you learn, and you grow. That is the only order in which sustainable confidence actually develops. Additionally, aim for excellence instead of perfection, and simply get started. Slowly, your competence will improve, your success ratio will soar, and genuine self-confidence will rise. But all of this positive growth can only happen if we first find the courage to try, warts and all.

Points to Ponder

How confident are you on a scale of 1-10 across various aspects in life? Explore the doubts and fears that hold you back from pursuing your dreams confidently. What are some tiny action steps you can commit to undertaking to go further in that confidence competence loop?

18

Stay Consistent

Many of us start and fail to pursue the path of personal growth and development, despite our best intentions, because we find it difficult to stay consistent. This journey is not for the fainthearted. We begin with great enthusiasm, but as time progresses, it becomes exhausting to keep at it. We feel overworked. We do not get enough sleep. Even our minds start making excuses that derail us from our intended path.

When we talk about self-transformation, it's important to recognise that it's not a one-time event; it's an ongoing process of growth and development. There are no limits to what we can learn and unlearn; the more we evolve, the more opportunities for growth emerge. Therefore, in this journey, what distinguishes winners from failures is consistent action. It is a crucial ingredient for fostering lasting change and propelling us toward a state of genuine well-being.

The key is to consistently put in the work and be patient, and the results will come soon enough. If we can keep our heads in the game and steadily progress towards our intentional goals, a day will come when we look back and hardly recognise ourselves.

What Impedes Consistency?

1. **Our Feelings**

   Our feelings are notoriously unreliable when it comes to driving change. Whenever we skip a workout or stray from our diet, we justify it by saying we didn't feel like exercising or had an insatiable craving for that sinfully delicious dish. Even our best intentions can be derailed by feelings that somehow never align with our goals. However, the truth is, we are never going to 'feel' like it.

   To put it simply, feelings are unreliable and temporary. We might feel lazy about going for a walk, and if we indulge that thought, we will experience momentary satisfaction. But that satisfaction quickly disappears and is replaced by guilt for not following through on our intentions. This sentiment is beautifully captured by the following quote:

   > 'Feelings come and go like clouds in a windy sky.'
   >
   > —Thich Nhat Hanh

   Remember that waiting for the right feeling will only hinder our progress and prevent us from attaining any remarkable achievement. Instead, we must let our actions dictate our mood, not the reverse.

2. **Lack of Confidence**

   Things like doubt, worry, and fear can also affect consistency. We cannot progress if we are constantly second-guessing ourselves, worrying about outcomes, or fearing that things won't unfold as expected. A lack of confidence in our abilities to achieve goals inevitably leads to faltering in the process.

In order to maintain consistency, we must tone down those inner voices of uncertainty and forge ahead with conviction. An unwavering belief in our capabilities, coupled with a steadfast commitment to our goals, empowers us to stay the course despite obstacles. Only then can we hope to turn our dreams into tangible realities through persistent, purposeful effort.

Remember the competence loop, confidence comes from trying, failing, and learning. No amount of intellectualising personal growth works. We have to get into the arena and play the game of life to learn what it takes to grow.

3. Eyes on the Prize

Another reason we falter is because we overemphasise the outcome, rather than keeping our eyes on the process. It's difficult to stay consistent when our minds are constantly fixated on the end goal or outcome without considering the steps required to get there.

An old Zen story illustrates this idea: A man approached a respected town monk, eager to attain the monk's state. He asked, 'How long will it take me to become like you?'

The monk deliberated and replied, 'Ten years.'

Unsatisfied, the man said, 'But what if I double my efforts? Surely it would take less time then?'

The monk responded, 'In that case, twenty years.'

Annoyed, the man argued, 'But I am promising to work harder. How could it take longer?'

The monk explained, 'If one eye focuses on the destination while the other watches the path, you'll take longer to arrive.'

To make steady progress swiftly, we need to keep both eyes on the road, which means all our awareness, thoughts, and energies should be directed toward the process. Consistency arises naturally when we commit to the path, not just the destination.

4. **All-or-nothing Mindset**

Often, we adopt an all-or-nothing approach from the get-go and then feel dejected at the first sign of failure. We are hard on ourselves, tolerating no mistakes. Such unrealistic expectations zap our motivation and momentum and set us up to fail each time.

However, we must realise that everyone must begin somewhere. We may encounter detours or make mistakes, but the point isn't to admonish ourselves and create fear of trying something new. The point is to learn from our missteps and figure out how to get back on track quickly. It is about learning to bounce back faster after every transgression by accepting imperfect action. One simple approach is to view every detour as a learning opportunity. When we see obstacles and roadblocks not as hindrances but as chances to discover and grow, the journey becomes smoother. Rather than viewing them as inconveniences, perceiving them as teachers in the game of life can help.

5. **Failed attempts in the past**

Humans naturally tend to label themselves. We may have tried things in the past and faltered, leading us to brand ourselves as undisciplined or inconsistent. We don't believe we have what it takes to succeed, reinforcing that belief through further failures.

However, our future need not mirror our past. Our future is what we choose to make of it. Instead of dwelling on past memories and wounds, we can focus our energy on why this goal matters now. How important is achieving it? What are the consequences of not succeeding? We must give ourselves a chance to forge a different path. The past only exists as memories; we can imprison our future in them or set ourselves free for a new beginning. Remember, we have the power to rewrite our life story. The choice to wield that power is ours.

6. **Negative Self-talk**

We all have an inner critic who judges us more harshly than our worst enemies. This critic berates us and never lets us forget our mistakes. At the first sign of faltering, our inner critic questions everything, and we direct unkind words at ourselves: 'Oh gosh, I'm so stupid', 'What was I thinking?', 'I'm good for nothing', 'I should just stop trying', and so on. We shame ourselves for not meeting our expectations, leading to disappointment.

Such critical self-talk can demotivate us from trying ever again. When we are embarking on a new way of life, that's the last thing we need. The importance of extending kindness and compassion to ourselves on the journey of personal growth cannot be emphasised enough. We need to be mindful of how we talk to and about ourselves because our subconscious is always listening. We want to imprint uplifting affirmations in our subconscious, not negative, limiting beliefs and fears. As we walk this path of self-improvement, we need kindness and empathy to stay anchored through life's journey.

How to Stay Consistent

To overcome the numerous obstacles to consistency discussed above, consider the following approaches:

1. **Make It Personal**

   Author James Clear beautifully explains that behaviour change happens at three levels: outcomes, processes, and identity. 'Outcomes are about what you get. Processes are about what you do. Identity is about who you wish to become. The ultimate form of intrinsic motivation is when a habit becomes part of your identity.'

   So, we can see that identity forms the core of lasting change. Instead of trying to inculcate something new, when we make habits part of our identity, they endure. For instance:

   - I don't just walk five times a day; I am someone who prioritises health.
   - I don't drink, socially or otherwise.
   - I am a reader, not someone who merely reads 15 minutes daily.

When habits sync with our identity, they become intrinsic. No longer needing external motivation, these behaviours happen automatically and consistently because they align with who we are at the core.

2. Hold Yourself Accountable

Most of us find consistency easier when accountable to someone else, be it bosses or family members. When we commit to others, consistency and self-accountability come naturally. But for personal goals and self-made commitments, consistency goes out the window. We set noble, well-meaning intentions for ourselves, but never follow through.

Why do we hold ourselves accountable to others' priorities but not our own? Some claim never finding time; others lacking energy; life getting in the way—illness, vacations, occasions, festivities becoming convenient excuses. Excuses abound, but the result is the same—we don't hold ourselves accountable. Eventually, years accumulate, and we feel regretful for never prioritising ourselves. By the time we wake up to what matters most, it's often too late, leaving a pile of regrets.

To stay consistent, ask yourself:

- First, are you undertaking this task because you truly want to, or based on what others around you are doing?
- Second, is it a priority for you *now*, given your other commitments?

- Third, do you value yourself and your personal ambitions enough to put in the work?

3. **Our Word Is Our Truth**

Many years ago, when I was unhappy with the way I was leading my life, one of the first things that stood out was how I would randomly utter words with no intention of following through. The subconscious guilt of not keeping my word eroded my confidence and self-esteem. Eventually, I began doubting my capabilities.

As humans, we may not leave behind much of a legacy, but in 2015 I realised the least I could do was keep my word, if not for others, then for myself. No more, no less. So, take the time to decide what you will do and who you want to become, measuring the words you utter as a commitment. Treat your word as the law and put it in action to make it happen, no matter what. By honouring your commitment, you will ensure that you remain consistent on your path.

4. **Keep It Aligned**

Even after making habits part of our identity and holding ourselves accountable, they won't last if our environment isn't conducive to our goals. The people we surround ourselves with and the ambience around us contribute to our success. If dieting, having tubs of ice cream and boxes of sweets readily available will undermine our progress and willpower. We must ensure our environment aligns with the habits and progress we want.

One approach is removing negative influences like treats when dieting or social media during 'deep focus' periods. Another is adding motivating elements representing our best selves, such as a vision board harnessing the power of visualisation or a photo of an admired role model. Humans instinctively elevate their behaviour when witnessed, and we can leverage this tendency as motivation for consistency.

As James Clear states, 'We tend to adopt habits praised by our culture because of our strong desire to fit in. One of the most effective things for building better habits is joining a culture where your desired behaviour is normal and you share something in common with the group.'

Moreover, in today's connected world, it's easier than ever to find and connect with like-minded communities vested in personal growth and conscious living. Regardless of our immediate surroundings, we can align ourselves with supportive online tribes. By aligning your environment and the people around you, friction towards desired goals reduces, and consistency becomes a natural consequence.

5. Prepare for Failure

When attempting something new, there will always be a chance we veer off course. We are human, after all, and our grand plans can fail. So, we might as well prepare for failure and have a plan for getting back on track afterwards. Creating a prevention plan from the start can help us prepare for that inevitable lapse in consistency and bounce back faster to continue progressing properly.

The first thing to remember is to never miss twice. Our first mistake never ruins the path, but repeated ones do. Often, after the first failure, we lose heart and give up. This is common with weight loss goals too! We start the week excited and motivated to diet and exercise. Then we find out there's an office lunch that Wednesday and our plans go haywire. We rationalise with ourselves saying we might as well start next week. And no prizes for guessing that the so-called next week never arrives. Instead of waiting for an opportune time when we can be 100 per cent consistent, it is vital to anticipate failure and have an action plan for when we falter. This reveals that staying consistent doesn't mean always hitting the bull's eye. Even if we miss the mark occasionally, that's okay; what's more important is aiming and shooting again.

6. An 'If-Then' Plan

For those trying to build habits they have previously failed at, this approach can work wonders. From past attempts, we can identify the events that sidetracked us from our original intentions. Instead of falling for them again, we can pre-emptively create a counter-plan using simple affirmation statements:

- If this <situation> happens, I will <do this> to correct it.
- If I indulge a craving and eat that dessert, then I will fast the next day to balance the calorie intake.

- If I don't have time to exercise due to long hours, then I will do 50 jumping jacks or a 1-minute plank.

Now you have backup plans for your goals. Though intensity may vary due to other responsibilities, using this approach, we can remain consistent in showing up for ourselves and our dreams.

7. Remember Your 'Why'

Another way to stay consistent is to remember why we started in the first place. Every time we intend to build a new habit or break an old one, we are preparing to fight autopilot tendencies and live life in a new way. The 'why' behind our intention is the fundamental driving force helping us inch closer to our goals, even if it's an uphill climb. Moreover, this 'why' is rooted in our past experiences and conditioning.

Taking time to understand the 'why' behind our intentions helps anchor us on the chosen path. Create a mental or physical visual reminder, like a note on your desk or phone wallpaper, to keep it top-of-mind. Our 'why' is what drives us to wake up each morning. Our 'why' pushes us to stand back up after every fall. Our 'why' compels us to show up consistently, no matter the circumstances.

8. One Day at a Time

Making grand statements like 'I will meditate every day for the rest of my life' sets us up for failure, when it's just a passing thought and too tall an order. However, there is another way: be consistent by taking it one day at a time. Wake up each morning and say to yourself, 'I will meditate today,' and follow through. It can be that simple.

No one can see the future. All we truly have is the present moment. Love it, live it fully! When we consistently make the right choice here and now, the future unfolds aligned with our actions. That's the way. Instead of forever plans, get today right. Do the next right thing every moment and brick by brick lay the foundations for an intentional life.

Points to Ponder

Remember, nothing changes unless you change what you do on a daily basis. Ask yourself what comes in the way of you being consistent towards your goals? Design a plan of action that will help you counter these obstacles and sustain your progress on the path of personal growth.

Part III
Beyond Fine

19
Going beyond Fine

Applying the principles covered in previous chapters can help us genuinely say, 'I am fine.' Meaning, that we achieve a state where we don't feel constantly in conflict with ourselves. There is an alignment between our thoughts, feelings, and actions. We feel more in control of our time, aware of every experience, and attuned to what feels right or wrong. We can catch ourselves when stressed, angry, or emotionally vulnerable and return to baseline sooner.

But is that enough? To me, certainly not. There has to be more to strive for. And indeed, there is.

It's a Process

Before embarking on the transformative journey from 'being fine' to something greater, it's important to understand that this is not a one-time event, but an ongoing process of unravelling and exploring new dimensions. It is a continuous journey of self-improvement, where the goal is not to compare ourselves to external milestones, but to look within and intentionally choose how to navigate the frictions of modern life with greater ease.

Going beyond 'fine' is not a fixed end state, but a continuous journey of self-discovery. The more we find ourselves, the more secure we feel within. The deeper we connect with those around us, the less resistance we create. The more compassionate we are towards ourselves, the more of that kindness and compassion radiate outwards.

This doesn't happen overnight or announce itself with pings and notifications. These shifts happen gradually and subtly. They are also not linear in progression. There would be times we regress back to autopilot ways of living. The key is self-awareness which includes paying attention to our thoughts, feelings, and experiences—how we respond when things go as planned versus when they don't. With time, we take full ownership of our lives and choose how to respond to stimuli around us, rather than reacting to every trigger.

Time to Move Ahead

We can go beyond being 'fine' and live a life of effortless ease—waking with a smile, having only love in our hearts, and maintaining equanimity through life's ups and downs. A life with little room for worry, stress, or anxiety, and where trust, self-belief, and faith reside. A life where we fall asleep peacefully without tossing and turning for hours, needing no escape or distraction. A life where we give and receive love freely. A life approaching each day with a sense of peace, joy, and bliss, knowing our true nature and purpose.

To achieve such a life, we need to expand the scope of who we can be. Beyond simply being 'fine,' there are additional states of being we could embody to attain a truly holistic existence. Let's explore what we can be.

20

Be Superhuman

Being human is super, says spiritual guru Sadhguru. As the most evolved beings on this planet, humans are inbuilt superhumans. We can think strategically, imagine, visualise, dream, and do so much more. The world today, for better or worse, is a testament to our intellectual prowess. But most of us are caught in the little games our minds play, rarely living in the real world. Our heads are filled with worries, and we are often imprisoned in self-imposed thinking traps. All our intelligence remains untapped when we continually suffer our minds. To go beyond fine, we need to realise our true nature, remind ourselves of our natural superpowers, and break the shackles of our fluctuating, limiting minds.

Indic scriptures cite ignorance or *avidya* as thc sourcc of this suffering. Ignorance of what? Of our true nature. The belief is that the moment we recognise our true nature, our sufferings can be controlled, managed, diminished, or removed entirely.

In the *Yoga Sutras,* Sage Patanjali further defines this avidya.

अनित्याशुचिदुःखानात्मसु नित्यशुचिसुखात्मख्यातिरविद्या I 2.5
(Ignorance is taking the impermanent, the impure, the painful, the non-self, as the eternal, the pure, the pleasurable and the self.)

Avidya or ignorance causes us to perceive:

- *Anitya* or impermanence as *nitya* or permanent. Consider our lives.
- *Asuci* or impurity as *suci* or purity. Think of our bodies and the effort we expend beautifying exteriors. If we could smell the chemicals within our bodies at any time, the stench would be unbearable.
- *Dukha* or misery as *sukha* or happiness. Consider that decadent seven-layer chocolate cake. It brings momentary happiness but can ultimately lead to diabetes, organ failure, and misery. Yet due to ignorance, we mistake fleeting sensory pleasures for lasting joy.
- *Anatmasu* or 'not self' as *atmakhyati* or Self. Think of our obsession with work, promotions, social status, wealth, and other insignificant aspects. This false knowledge inhibits us from seeing ourselves as we truly are.

Much of our suffering stems from total identification with material objects and the world around us. We continue believing happiness lies in the next promotion, our children's success, growing social status or wealth—only to realise that elusive happiness remains out of reach. We attach our identity and self-worth to things like employment status, marital status, and finances, and the smallest shift destabilises our entire lives.

We obsess over our limited existence, constantly planning and trying to control our environment to feel safe. We live in a precarious world where tomorrow's uncertainty is scary. All our planning is an attempt to avoid being caught off guard, to prepare for any eventuality so we can remain safe and unscathed.

But we must realise that no amount of preparation can provide a true sense of safety. There are and always will be circumstances beyond our imagination that can and will occur because that is the nature of life. Rather than feeling overwhelmed by possibilities beyond our control, we need to rein in our fear and make peace with 'not knowing.'

We often speak of the fear of the unknown. But as philosopher Jiddu Krishnamurti beautifully stated, 'No one can be afraid of the unknown because that is something we do not even know.' The fear is not of what the future unknown brings, but of losing what is known, the familiar and comfortable. Fear stems from the uncertainty of security, the unwillingness to detach or let go. In a nutshell, our pleasure-seeking minds think and seek certainty in an uncertain world. This is neither plausible nor practical. The sooner we clarify this ignorance and realise our true nature, the less we will suffer.

Meditation: A Tool to Unlock Infinite Potential

Meditation is not some new discovery; its roots trace back thousands of years when ancient sages and spiritual leaders recognised its profound power to harmonise the mind, body, and spirit. It's transcendental nature to take us beyond our worldly realities and connect us with a higher force residing right within us.

Many practices have died a natural death over the centuries but not meditation, because it's still as relevant if not more in our chaotic and confusing times. However, like many things that become popular, its essence has diluted significantly in the last decade. In the age of social media ads, meditation has been trivialised as a solution to reduce stress, anxiety, overwhelm, and to find calm and quiet. It does all of this, yes! But it can offer much, much more.

Meditation was primarily prescribed as a means for liberation. But it offers countless benefits even for those not spiritually inclined. Let's explore. Many of us today suffer from decision paralysis or analysis paralysis, which meditation addresses and more. It helps us gain clarity and insight, allowing us to operate from inner wisdom and see through our ignorance or delusion. It enables us to be fully present and experience life more vividly. Meditation also helps nurture focus and deepen concentration but more importantly, it helps us come to terms with what is, irrespective of external circumstances.

Now that we have delved into the numerous benefits of meditation, let's closely examine its meaning.

What Is Meditation?

Often when we hear the word 'meditation,' we picture a monk sitting in uncomfortable postures for long periods. Misconceptions such as these often create a barrier to approaching meditation in contemporary society. Personally, I find Buddhist monk Shinzen Young's straightforward definition more relatable: 'Any situation where you are consciously cultivating focus is, by definition, a meditation.'

In other words, we can say that meditation is an act of paying attention. In our distraction-filled world, the skill of paying attention is overlooked. Meditation serves as a tool to disconnect from these distractions, allowing us to focus and observe our inner experiences. As we become witnesses to thoughts, feelings, and sensations arising and passing, we create space within ourselves. However, sustaining this state requires continuous practice of observation.

To meditate effortlessly, we must not try to forcibly stop our thoughts, as that is futile. Continually commanding ourselves to 'stop thinking' only generates another thought, plunging us into a relentless cycle.

The path we need to pursue is that of letting go. Instead of riding the waves of every passing thought, we need to simply sit by the shore as witnesses, watching, and feeling. Allow the waves of thoughts to arise and manifest as they will, without grasping onto them. By being a mere observer, neither resisting nor feeding the thoughts, they will eventually fade away on their own accord.

How Long Should You Meditate?

Meditation needn't be a 10-minute morning affair on yoga mats. We can infuse every aspect of life with the essence of meditation. By bringing our complete attention and consciousness to whatever we do, we can naturally embody a meditative state.

As you engage in daily activities, do so with utmost awareness. When you read, immerse yourself fully in the words on the page. With each step you take, be present in the moment. While eating, savour each bite mindfully. And in moments of joy and celebration, embrace the experience with all your senses. By honing our focus in this way, we gradually disentangle ourselves from distractions and gain clearer insights into reality. Through sustained practice, we start to perceive the eternal, untainted aspects of existence that offer genuine and enduring happiness. As the veil of ignorance lifts, a select few may even catch a glimpse of their true, extraordinary nature. Embark on the journey of meditation today to unlock the potential of your innate superhuman self.

21

Be Present

Another aspect of our being that can elevate us beyond the mundane is presence. Our complete, undivided presence has the power to enhance the quality and richness of every little thing we encounter in life. But the reality is that we are seldom truly present in the here and now.

We may be physically at work, but mentally our minds are drifting to a deserted island in the Maldives. Emotionally, we replay old wounds from the past. We are neither fully here nor there. Constantly thinking about what went wrong before or anxiously planning for some future event, we oscillate between the past and future, missing out on this present moment—the only place where real life is actually unfolding.

As author Myrko Thum insightfully stated, 'Everything that happens, happens in the present moment. Everything that ever happened and will ever happen can only happen in the present moment. It is impossible for anything to exist outside of it.'

If we navigate through life without being fully present, even if we achieve great success, we will find ourselves feeling empty inside. Genuine satisfaction and the exhilaration of achievement stem from a different realm altogether—one characterised by undivided attention, steadfast focus, and wholehearted dedication. It's a realm of absolute 'presence.'

Have you experienced losing track of time and space when utterly immersed in a task before you? Today we call it the 'flow state,' but essentially it occurs when all our concentration and focus rests on what we are doing at that very moment. So complete is our absorption that the usual separation between doer, object, and action dissolves. Our sense of self, the ego, fades away as we become one with the activity. As you read these very words, how present are you to the knowledge you are consuming? What sorts of thoughts currently run in the back of your mind?

To be present does not require a huge effort. On the contrary, presence arises when we simply let go and lose ourselves in the task at hand. All we need to do is make the conscious choice to be attentive in every little thing we do. When we wake and brush our teeth, feel the bristles, the grip of the toothbrush in hand. When sitting for breakfast, feel the body's weight on the chair, and experience the explosion of flavours and spices with each morsel. Follow this presence in routine after routine until we fall asleep. It is easier said than done but we must persist.

Use an Anchor

Given how easily distracted our minds are by nature, it may be difficult to simply stop the churn of thoughts and forcibly pay attention to the present moment. Instead, we can use an anchor to gently bring us back at frequent intervals. This could be setting a singing bowl alarm on your phone to chime every hour or placing a visual cue in your workspace or home to remind you to return to the here and now.

Another powerful way to anchor ourselves is to use the one constant happening within our bodies that we can easily observe—the breath. Focusing on the breath is a remarkably effective tool for improving moment-to-moment presence.

Whenever we catch our mind wandering, simply turning our attention to the inhale and exhale can help us re-engage with the task at hand. It requires conscious effort in the beginning. But when we persistently use this technique, it becomes a habit. We don't need to change what we do. We need only to change our ways of living to become more consciously aware of each moment.

22
Be Kind

Most of us reading this may have kindness and compassion for the people around us but seldom is that generosity extended inwardly to ourselves. Many of us spend lifetimes loathing and resenting who we are at our core. We hold up some false ideal of who we 'should' be, either wrongly presumed by ourselves or imprinted since childhood. Every time we fail to live up to those unrealistic expectations, we feel disappointment, giving rise to self-hatred.

The important point to understand here is that no amount of meaningful work in the external world will help us transcend a 'just fine' state if we are constantly judging ourselves harshly. To be truly compassionate with ourselves requires 100 per cent radical self-acceptance. When we can wholeheartedly accept every part of who we are—our strengths, weaknesses, failures, desires, pleasant or unpleasant qualities—all of it, then living our best lives becomes the natural consequence. We must truly own every aspect of ourselves to feel secure in our own skin and arrive at a level of comfort with where we are today before we can envision an evolved version that goes beyond the ordinary.

The unfortunate truth is that most of us are our own worst critics. Consciously or not, we keep getting in our own way, sabotaging progress with limiting beliefs and false narratives drawn from past experiences. Shirzad Chamine, author and founder of *Positive Intelligence,* identifies ten saboteurs that hijack our thoughts and emotions. Among them, he argues that we all share one master saboteur—the Judge. We each harbour this ruthless inner critic who constantly judges and criticises everything we think or do. It is this saboteur that holds us back from attempting big things in life, for fear of failure or embarrassment.

From Critique to Compassion

We are all born with a clean slate and with time and through every experience in life, we form impressions, add inferences, and build defence mechanisms to survive and protect ourselves from whatever threats we perceive in our environment. We had to toughen up to survive, and so we did. But as adults, we may find that not all of those defences still serve us or are needed. Rather, they weigh us down unnecessarily. However, by that point those defence mechanisms have become interwoven into our very identities, making them tricky to disassociate from. We keep labelling and limiting ourselves to small, narrow spaces when we can be and are, in fact, so much more!

Such defence mechanisms are understandable if life is entirely cyclical and repetitive. If what's going to happen in the future is merely the same as what happened in our past. But that's not true, is it? Imagine how boring life would be if only what occurred before could reoccur endlessly! The creator did not craft such a stagnant, tedious universe. But when we box ourselves into limiting beliefs and labels, we unconsciously let our lives be dictated by past experiences rather than future possibilities.

Remember, we are spiritual beings having a human experience, and not the other way around. This means we are not these narrowly limited humans defined solely by personality, but spiritual beings temporarily having a human experience. So, let's not judge ourselves so harshly by how we have fared in the past. Instead, let's accept ourselves for all that we are and all that we are not, and truly love ourselves with every fibre of our being.

Limitless possibilities open up when we stop standing in the way of our own progress. Transformation then comes from a place of love and compassion towards self, not hate, anger, and resentment. By accepting our imperfections, and loving ourselves in all our quirks and behaviours, we open up greater avenues for growth and evolution. And when we connect with our true nature, self-acceptance and self-love become our intuitive way of being.

Now let's look at some ways we can nurture self-love.

Change the Self-talk

One powerful way to move towards self-acceptance and self-love is to deepen our self-awareness and be mindful of the internal conversations we have with ourselves. As mentioned earlier, we all harbour a critical inner voice that judges us far more harshly than any sworn enemy ever could. We need to tame this inner judge and treat ourselves with the same kindness and compassion that we readily extend to those we love.

For instance, how do we speak to ourselves when we make a mistake? Is it with love, gentleness, and understanding?

Would we address a dear friend in the same berating manner when they make a similar mistake? How can we become more mindful of this internalised self-talk?

The way we talk to ourselves can make or irreparably break us. We can build ourselves up through positive self-talk or crush any seed of potential with negativity. By becoming more aware of how we internally speak to ourselves, we can learn to accept both our strengths and weaknesses with equanimity. Remember, our self-talk wields profound power to nurture self-love and radical acceptance or perpetuate merciless self-judgement. The choice lies with us.

Drop the Narratives

Another powerful technique to cultivate self-love is to untangle past experiences and disassociate from inferences that are no longer valid or serving us. Journalling is a great way to process past experiences, heal, and grow through such self-reflection. Experiment with regularly journalling your thoughts and emotions and observe the repeated patterns and stories you tend to tell yourself. Over time, validate those stories against facts, and let go of any fictitious tales periodically. As we shed these unnecessary layers, we can start moving closer towards being our own best friends.

If our self-perception is clouded by self-hatred, a great way to clear that fog is to gain perspective on how others see us. Ask people you trust about how they perceive you. Often, we are blinded by our own deep-seated convictions and beliefs about ourselves. External observers may have differing worldviews or perspectives from which we can gather more data on who else we are. This widens our notion of who we are and helps us find more inner peace.

The beauty is that change can start to happen almost instantaneously, as soon as we move towards complete acceptance of our whole selves. As the renowned psychologist Carl Rogers said, 'The curious paradox is that when I accept myself just as I am, then I can change.' When we stop fighting against who we truly are, we open up vast possibilities for positive transformation.

All in all, to truly transcend being just 'fine' and live our best lives, we must be kind to ourselves first, and learn to be our own compassionate companions on this journey.

23
Be Child-like

We enter this world as peaceful, blissful beings. In our initial years, we are joyous, curious, and brimming with energy despite not understanding life's ways. From that default state of joy, we grow up defaulting to unhappiness. The reason for this is that our early childhood experiences condition us, changing something within that makes it harder to be our true selves. With every negative or unpleasant experience, we develop defence mechanisms to avoid such situations. We cage parts of ourselves under lock and key, perceiving them as threats unhelpful for surviving on this planet.

Yet to truly live our best lives, we need to heal those inner child wounds and become whole again. When our inner child is crushed and dispirited, we cannot fully open ourselves to embrace life's entirety. We need to be whole and complete to open up and receptively experience all the universe's goodness. As author Brennan Manning says, 'When our inner child is not nurtured and nourished, our minds gradually close to new ideas, unprofitable commitments and the surprises of the spirit.'

Therefore, we must set our inner child free by releasing it from the crushing weight of the world it has taken on over the years. We must heal these wounds that crushed our spirit and reignite the joyous inner child within. The fact of the matter is our inner child needs love, kindness, unconditional acceptance, and a safe space to be wild, untamed, and free. But first, we must acknowledge our inner child. That is Step 1. Connect and accept its current state. Acknowledge the pain, scars, and wounds, and see the ways we have crushed its spirit.

Step 2 includes addressing the wounds by engaging that inner child in conversation. Discuss the fear, guilt, unreasonable expectations of perfection, recurring anxiety, anger, or resentfulness. Process the emotions. Write letters to your inner child, release the overwhelming weight of unfulfilled expectations through meditation, and mend things in the best way possible. If those who caused the wounds are alive, converse with them and explain how they made you feel, without expecting an apology. The purpose is to find more inner peace, not hold grudges or resentment toward those who triggered defensive responses in your childhood.

Then it's time for Step 3 which entails returning to being your genuine self. Offer safety, comfort, and reassurance. Remind yourself that you are an adult now, not a helpless toddler. You can better care for the inner child's needs. Embrace everything about your inner child and invite it back into your life. Find ways to recapture childhood joys daily, no matter how small.

Connecting with Your Inner Child

Were you a non-stop dancer as a kid? A compulsive doodler? The expressive writer articulating life's absurdities? Was fantasy fiction your passion? Or crafting from scraps of paper? Whatever it was, integrate the things you loved when you were a child back into your present life. Even if it's for just ten minutes daily, try to make some time for it. Allow self-expression without judgement. Channel that inner child, your life guide. This aspect was perfectly articulated by musician-author Stephen Nachmanovitch, 'The most potent muse of all is our own inner child.'

We often view muses as arbitrary concepts, but the truth is they are within each of us. We need only open up and allow self-expression without scrutiny, censorship, or judgment. This lets our inner child thrive. When our inner child thrives, we are at ease within, and this ease is invaluable in helping us go beyond fine.

24
Be Generous

Humans are inherently ambitious. Since time immemorial, we have desired to explore and conquer lands and seas far and wide. As children, we did this by seeing, touching, feeling, or even tasting and chewing objects, simply wanting to know our environments intimately. As adults, we aim to conquer professional worlds and acquire more material comforts—bigger houses, SUVs, luxury cars, watches, large TVs, or the latest smartphones. Most of us get stuck in this loop, with barely enough time to fulfil unending material desires, never thinking beyond.

But if we have chased material pleasures even briefly, we might have experienced dissonance. Beyond a certain threshold, the additional satisfaction from more possessions doesn't feel worth the effort. With each new acquisition, we feel lesser satisfaction and fulfilment. That's because a deeper force within us craves more than just material comforts. This peace can only be attained by giving.

Why Generosity Matters

Why is it important to go beyond our selfish needs, you may ask? The reason is simple. Unselfish acts are difficult. They go against our animalistic instincts and by giving without expecting anything in return, we overcome the narrow, petty-minded animal consciousness and move towards higher consciousness.

As Swami Vivekananda says, 'The degree of unselfishness marks the degree of success everywhere.' Practising this is straightforward. Find an avenue to contribute without the expectation of receiving anything. Something that brings meaning and fulfilment. An act engaged in solely for the sake of doing it. Experiment and see what you are called to give.

Having a larger-than-life selfless desire is a great driving force to wake up every day looking forward to making a difference. It is a powerful way to go beyond just being 'fine' in our lives, to truly make meaningful contributions through our lifetime that serve a wider common purpose besides ourselves.

Generosity Is Soul Food

Material comforts may enhance individual quality of life, but it's important to recognise that inner spirit is not dualistic and separate from the universe. The soul craves meaning and fulfilment by doing good for the collective. The soul finds meaning by serving universal well-being.

The Spanish painter Pablo Picasso profoundly stated, 'The meaning of life is to find your gift. The purpose of life is to give it away.' The word 'purpose' is often misused in modern life contexts, where the hunt for a purpose has become a rat race in itself. But we each have something unique to contribute. We each arrive bearing gifts only we can bring, and we do the world a disservice by not allowing their expression.

For some, this could be their profession; the daily work being their way of giving back and contributing. For others, work might be purely commercial intent to afford desired lifestyles. In that case, identify ways to channel unique strengths—perhaps counselling financial investing if skilled with finances, or giving the gift of music to neighbourhood children if blessed with a remarkable voice. It also needn't necessarily be for humans. For example, giving back could mean caring for strays or planting trees around the city.

Remember what we give matters less than why we give it. Being of service towards something greater than survival needs automatically elevates the quality of our life.

25

Be Balanced

A common way we drain our energies is when we keep fluctuating between extreme opposites. We work gruelling 18-hour days for 6 weeks straight and then escape to Bali for 5 days to reset. We starve ourselves with fad diets, only to binge eat. Every time we wildly swing from one extreme to the other, we lose momentum and drain our energies in vain. Instead, if we could hold steady to the middle ground, find our centred balance, and stay rooted there, we could avoid this endless cycle of depletion. By staying centred or balanced, we can navigate the many ups and downs of life with greater ease, finding that sustainable middle path.

The significance of maintaining this delicate balance becomes evident while working with a potter's wheel. When moulding clay, we are instructed not to apply too much pressure. We need to grip the clay and shape it with a gentle, controlled touch. If we hold too loosely, we cannot give form to the clay. Too much force and it breaks apart. This valuable lesson in pottery is also deeply applicable to how we live.

This is not some New-Age spiritual teaching. In the Bhagavad Gita, Lord Krishna himself states the following lines in Chapter 6, Verse 17:

युक्ताहारविहारस्य युक्तचेष्टस्य कर्मसु |
युक्तस्वप्नावबोधस्य योगो भवति दु:खहा ||17||

The verse roughly translates as follows:

'For the disciplined person, whose consumption and recreation are regulated, whose exertion in actions is properly balanced, whose sleep and wakefulness are regulated—yoga becomes the destroyer of pain.' Simply put, those who are balanced in their eating, recreation, work efforts, sleep, and wakefulness become the 'slayer of sorrows'.

This same wisdom was echoed many millennia later by Gautama Buddha, when he urged individuals to walk the middle path; a path characterised neither by complete abstinence nor by excessive indulgence. It is said that during Buddha's own journey toward enlightenment, he went through a phase of giving up eating and drinking entirely in order to meditate without interruption. However, within days his body grew weak and dizzy, making meditation next to impossible. At that time, he overheard some village women singing, with lyrics loosely translating to 'Tighten the strings of the *tanpura* (lute). But do not tighten them so much that the strings break.' Upon hearing these words, he immediately realised he should nourish and strengthen his body, and not go to such an extreme that the body itself is destroyed.

In our fast-paced modern lives, excess has become the name of the game. Technology has unlocked new levels of sensory indulgence with 10-minute deliveries offering the world at our doorstep. Work has insidiously seeped into every waking moment through calls at odd hours, constant

Teams notifications and WhatsApp pings. To truly live our best lives, we need to find that elusive balance between work and play, action and rest, doing and simply being.

26

Build Meaningful Connections

In today's hyperconnected world, where we are virtually linked to millions globally via pocket-sized devices, we have never been lonelier. A 2021 survey revealed that 33 per cent of adults globally experienced loneliness, and in India, that number was 43 per cent—nearly one in every two adults feeling lonely in one of the world's most densely populated countries.

We need to understand that humans are social beings first. We managed to dominate earth not because we were the fastest or strongest, but due to our ability to collaborate in large numbers for shared collective purposes. Historian Yuval Noah Harari states, 'Ants and bees can also work together in huge numbers, but very rigidly and only with close relatives. Wolves and chimpanzees cooperate far more flexibly but only with small numbers they know intimately. Sapiens can cooperate extremely flexibly with countless strangers. That's why sapiens rule the world, while ants eat our leftovers and chimps are locked in zoos and labs.'

Our ancestors belonged to large communities where help, companionship, and camaraderie were readily available. Trust was the foundation keeping clans together, helping them survive unfavourable conditions. But over time, the unit we call 'family' has shrunk. Today's nuclear families have few connections, posing a real threat. We feel disconnected from those around us. We can have thousands of online connections, but they don't offer the same security as meaningful, real relationships.

In order to live beyond just 'fine,' we must invest time and effort in cultivating meaningful relationships. We need tribes with which to share honestly, seek support, and lend a supportive shoulder selflessly without envy or insecurity. And this begins with us—being honest, vulnerable, trustworthy, and respectful. Asking for help unhesitatingly, offering whatever help we can generously, and, letting go of grudges that no longer serve us, wishing nothing but the best for all. Adventurer Christopher McCandless captured this sentiment immaculately: 'Happiness is only real when shared.'

It is essential to realise that love is the secret ingredient coursing through our veins, making every moment beautiful. We are often taught young to treat strangers with suspicion, loving only those close. As we grow, we must ensure our ability to love expands. Before that, it is important to begin with unconditional acceptance for our inner circles. Experience that selfless love state, then slowly expand it outward—to neighbours, service workers, teachers, shopkeepers, etc. Be loving in all conversations, even with strangers. Love regardless of nationality, caste, creed, or religion.

Soon, there will come a time when we are no more, so before then, tell those you cherish how much you loved, cared for, and learned from them, how they mattered, and how they are part of you as you are of them. What's the point of holding all that love in our hearts? Why not share it generously?

Expand Your Circle of Compassion

If we treated everyone the way we would like to be treated, the world would be a far kinder place. If we struggle to care for someone, try the following simple visualisation exercise.

Imagine how the person you want to extend your love to looked as a joyous three or four-year-old before being conditioned into their current way of being. See the pure light they were, the twinkle in their eyes. We cannot be angry at that child. When being loving becomes our inner nature, very little can move us from our anchor. We won't be swayed by insecurities, jealousy, or anger. We will genuinely care for others' well-being.

We cannot pursue larger-than-life dreams without loving and caring for those around us. Chasing dreams for a cause greater than personal needs requires feeling compassion for others. And when we hold unconditional love for humankind, there is no limit to what we can achieve. We serve and feel that sense of belonging to a larger community, going beyond just being 'fine' is a natural consequence.

By transforming our being and doing through these ways, we will lead lives that far transcend fine. We learn to truly thrive, recognise the endless possibilities, and live our best lives.

27

Stop Deferring Life

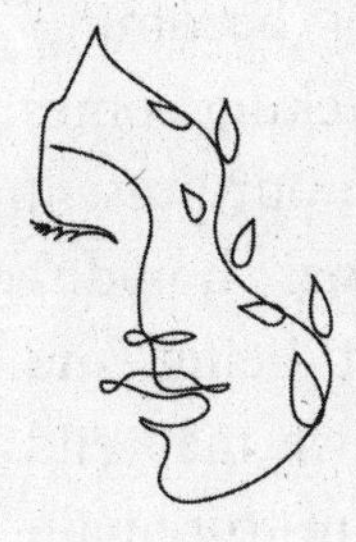

Consider this thought: 'I will live my best life when I have X amount of rupees in the bank, become a partner at that firm, my startup goes public, or I finally settle into a relationship.' Or let's take another scenario: 'I will have the time of my life when I lose those extra kilos, my children grow up and settle down, or once I retire peacefully.'

However, the truth is that such milestones are endless. As life evolves, goals change, and we keep running from one accomplishment to the next, only to reach the end empty-handed. Life slips away in this incessant chase for more and a better tomorrow never arrives, and these milestones are lies we tell ourselves. As Indian-American entrepreneur Naval Ravikant says that desires are contracts we make with ourselves to be unhappy until then. Thus, it is essential to realise that there is no tomorrow, and the only thing we can do is seize the day and live life fully in this very moment. It's foolish to postpone living for that uncertain future.

It's also important to note that there's nothing wrong with desires or ambition, but they must not come at the cost of present happiness. If our desires leave us miserable in the moment, something is wrong. Happiness isn't found someplace else or in the future, but right here, right now. We need to find joy in being where we are and be at peace with exactly who we are today. Instead of deferring to some future when all desires are fulfilled, we need to learn to live now.

Similarly, we shouldn't wait to be our best versions before living our best lives. It's great to be aware we are works-in-progress, but we often get stuck in the loop of 'becoming' and forget to live in the meantime. Constant seeking comes at a heavy price—persistent dissatisfaction with our present state. It is good to aspire for better, but the goal shouldn't dominate every waking second. If our present 'being' and aspirations of 'becoming' constantly conflict, we may end up worse off than before. Rather, we should aim to remain present, enjoying each moment where the magic lies, while consciously aspiring to be a little better each day.

When we accept where we are today, make peace with not knowing tomorrow, find joy in the process, and strive to be 1 per cent better than yesterday, we will start leading lives of effortless ease.

28
Embrace Mortality

We can transcend just being 'fine' by cultivating acute awareness of our mortality. In Stoic philosophy, almost every discourse on living a good life is incomplete without addressing our mortality and inevitable death. From Epictetus, who advocated a 'nearness to death' so that we always maintain proper perspective and never desire more than the bare essentials, to Seneca, who urged us to mentally prepare each moment as if it were the end of our lives. And Marcus Aurelius argued that a man's life is fleeting and small in the grand cosmos, and even a hunger for posthumous legacy fades quickly, known by few who will themselves soon perish. Thus, we can see how mortality is the central driving theme for many prominent and historical figures.

An important point to note here is that this is not some morbid obsession with death or wanting to outlast our mortal lives to leave an enduring legacy behind. It is about coming to terms with the only absolute certainty we have—that we come with an expiration date. We can whine and resist or use that truth as a whip to push us into living our best lives now. The fact is that nothing hits as sobering as truly grappling with our mortality. We are born, we live, and we die; this is the inescapable nature of this life. But most of us walk around acting as if we have all the time in the world to live. There is no urgency, no intensity, no vitality. So, to live a rich, meaningful life, we must first stop denying the possibility of our impermanence and mortality.

The Dalai Lama speaks profoundly when asked what most surprises him about humanity. He answered, 'Man! Because he sacrifices his health in order to make money. Then he sacrifices money to recuperate his health. And then he is so anxious about the future that he does not enjoy the present; the result being that he does not live in the present or the future; he lives as if he is never going to die, and then dies having never really lived.' Growing up in an era with so much taboo around death, we have been conditioned to pretend that the one certainty in our lives is not even a possibility. We are afraid to even utter the word, as if not saying it will make it not happen. But denying death means denying life itself.

Keeping the inevitable end in perspective can motivate us to make the absolute most of every fleeting moment. Death reminds us of the temporary nature of all experiences we encounter in this life and helps us gain healthy detachment when things don't go our way. A friendly mortality check can help us live more intentionally by nudging us to prioritise what will matter most on our deathbeds.

It's time we recognise life and death are inextricably intertwined. Only when we come to terms with our mortality can we truly say an impassioned 'yes' to this gift of life.

Death as a Catalyst for Positive Change

Asking yourself each morning, 'What would I do if today were the last day of my life?' is a powerful way to remember our mortality. This questioning helps put our problems and habitual complaining into healthy perspective, while instilling a vital sense of urgency to make the most of the time we have. Also, instead of being afraid, remembering our mortality can inspire us to bring that urgency into our daily lives. Accepting the reality of death makes us more inspired to live fully, be utterly present, and ensure every moment counts.

The truth is that no mythical tomorrow will swoop in to magically fulfil all our dreams. All we are granted is today, this very moment. And this is simultaneously a precious gift and a sobering reminder of our limits. Let us not foolishly waste away this gift in petty arguments, bitter resentment, fear, or laziness. Instead, let's use the prompt of our finitude each day to live a life that genuinely matters while we can.

Death can be the driving force that inspires us to urgently savour and maximise every breath we are given on this wondrous, fleeting journey of being alive. When we embrace our mortality, we embrace life itself in its fullness.

29

FIND JOY IN LITTLE THINGS

Have you seen a serious baby? Isn't their default state one of joy, pleasantness, and playfulness? One reason we never transcend just 'fine' as adults is that we take life too seriously—our work, relationships, career growth, financial status, social standing, and our very selves.

It's vital to realise that we have but a brief journey here, where all is temporary. The little things we worry about rarely occur, and even if they do, their impact is insignificant in the grand scheme. Instead of taking things so seriously, we can breathe easy and find joy in the mundane, everyday moments. Yet we only celebrate life in pockets—first breaks, big raises, bucket-list vacations, dream weddings, childbirths, and other milestones. Why hunt for reasons to celebrate? Aren't the ordinary moments of health, aliveness, and breathing enough to celebrate?

We cherish the ordinary only when temporarily lost or taken away—through illness, distance from family, or losing someone dear without ever expressing how much they meant. Then we realise the value of ordinary things. Think of that pre-dawn breath of fresh air. Tight hugs. Loved ones' sparkling smiles. A warm cup of coffee. Shared laughs over inside jokes at inappropriate times. A glorious lakeside sunset. A pain-free body. The earth's aroma as rain falls. The fight for that delicious cake's last bite. The shoulders we leaned on when times got tough. Tiny miracles and coincidences. The simple reassuring touch says all will be okay in the end. That reassuring twinkle. The sound of waves rising and crashing. The stillness of inaction. Random acts of kindnesses from strangers.

What if we realised and cherished these small yet immensely fulfilling moments as they happened, not just when they are taken away? How glorious would it be to live without being caught in the vicious cycle of wanting? By learning to see the extraordinary in the ordinary, we can live peacefully and joyfully despite external circumstances. We can reignite the childlike wonder of experiencing each moment fully. Pour our hearts into each day. Allow nature to leave us speechless whenever we are surrounded by it. Have a spring in our step from morning till night. Breathe through your incessant worries and thoughts. Playfully shake off petty anxieties, trusting we are eternally protected. When we find joy in the little things, life feels more fulfilling.

30
Embrace Life's Ups and Downs

By now, we have experienced that there is an inherent ebb and flow to life. Meaning, there are periods when we fly high and move at rocket speed through life's many adventures, and there are periods when we lay low, barely inching along through sticky situations. While we tend to gracefully sail through periods of energetic flow, we remain profoundly uncomfortable with the ebbs. The downswings feel unnatural because we have been fed utopian narratives of perpetual productivity since childhood.

We grow up imbibing those unreasonable expectations of ourselves. We expect to churn out measurable output every single hour, like an assembly line in a factory. But we are not finely calibrated machines, are we? We are dynamic thinking, feeling human beings who cannot simply operate like a robot on command. Our unrealistic expectations set us up for a constant sense of failure because we can never live up to that level of robotic efficiency.

Perhaps during the agricultural and industrial eras, it made sense to narrowly measure an individual's worth by their output generated per unit of time invested. But in today's internet-powered knowledge era, our value needs to be measured by the ingenuity of our thoughts and creativity, not merely the volume of output generated. Regardless, we still cling to these outdated metrics of self-evaluation, finding ourselves spiralling into existential crisis whenever we get stuck in life's inevitable ebbs.

To truly live a life beyond 'fine,' we need to let go of these unrealistic and unhealthy standards. We need to understand that there will be periods when we lay fallow and restore, and other times when we will fly high in inspired states of flow. We can neither afford to catastrophise and sink into existential crisis with every ebb, nor forget our deeper 'why' while manically riding the productive highs. We need to stay anchored to our core values, our driving purpose, and our authentic selves through the dynamic ebbs and flows of life.

Regular Check-ins

For a more realistic expectation of productivity, we need to stay connected with our internal state—our thoughts, emotions, and energy levels. A helpful practice is to have regular check-ins with ourselves to consciously connect with the condition of our body and mind. This allows us to assess how energised and aligned we truly feel on any given day. This can include asking yourself the following questions each morning: 'How is my body feeling today?', 'How is my mind?', and 'What are my overall energy levels?'

We need to understand that as human beings, we don't feel precisely the same way every day or even every hour. Checking in with ourselves frequently can help gauge whether we have the necessary bandwidth to fully engage with the tasks we have planned. Based on it, we can modify our workload to match the actual energy and motivation levels available that day. Flexibly adjusting our to-do list to align with our authentic state of being helps us operate more intelligently. Do note that this isn't about making excuses to avoid difficult things, but a smarter way to harmonise our efforts with our energy.

All in all, in today's world where most of us are knowledge workers relying on our intellect, creativity, and intuition, we need to redesign productivity metrics that allow us to generate high-quality work effortlessly. We must also remember that both the ebbs and flows of life are natural and transient and neither will last forever. The good times and the difficult ones will both pass. The pleasure and the pain, the joy and the miseries—all of it will pass in due course. All we need to do is remain equanimous throughout the shifting tides.

31

Don't Settle for Mere Existence

If there's only one thing you take away from this book, let it be this: Never settle for anything but the best in this precious life. If you are unhappy, discontent, and frustrated, stay with that until clarity emerges, and then make the necessary shifts happen. If your life is feeling like a relentless drag, instead of sticking to the miserable status quo and wallowing, question what's missing and work towards plugging that gap. If you are stressed and anxious all the time, make changes or find healthy ways to deal with it, rather than allowing that undercurrent to poison the most vital decades of your life. If you are always angry or resentful, address the root causes and nip them in the bud, rather than allowing them to fester and poison you from within. If you are sad and depressed, reach out to friends and family or seek professional help to reframe your perspective, rather than remaining lost and stuck in a prison of your own mind's making. If you are unhappy in a relationship, build a support system to work on it genuinely. If it still doesn't improve, then walk away with your head held high.

Let's not wait until we hit rock bottom to realise that we have always had the power to transform our lives. Instead of playing the victim, let's take complete responsibility and work towards moulding our lives to our highest satisfaction. Let's permit ourselves to dream boldly, to love ourselves and those around us wholeheartedly, to make peace with the great unknown, to be wild and free, to have the courage to ask for the moon and then go get it.

Imagine if we allowed continued self-awareness and consciousness to be our wake-up call, rather than diseases, accidents, or some kind of loss forcing us to make the necessary changes in our lives. All that is required is tiny positive changes every single day and being curious about how to live bigger, better and fuller. As the wise Albus Dumbledore said: 'Help will always be given . . . to those who ask for it.'

Set aside the ifs, buts, maybes, shoulds and what-ifs; seize the profound moment, every single day. Take those chances, make those delicious mistakes, say yes to those crazy adventures, look ridiculous, be kind, forgive others, smile a lot more, love generously, and live a lot more expansively. Do not settle for second-rate existence in this fleeting gift of life. Remember, now is all we are guaranteed, and this time will never roll around again. It is up to us to make it count while we can.

Acknowledgements

The entire universe had to conspire to bring this book into existence. Here is a brief mention of just some of the people I am immensely grateful towards for making this journey so worthwhile.

To Thatha, who always appreciated the art of good writing and helped me realise the power of words from a tender age. Thank you for sowing those seeds of a writer within me so early on. I hope you will approve of this book, wherever you may be now.

To Amma and Appa, for their countless sacrifices to ensure my sister and I had the privileged opportunity to freely pursue our dreams.

To Sowmya, for being my forever partner in crime. For steadfastly being there through all the highs and lows, including the writing of this book.

To Saswat, for being my anchor, making me burst into laughter even in the most inappropriate moments, and for lovingly making an exception to read this before I released it to the world.

I would like to express my gratitude to my family by marriage for always being so supportive and encouraging.

I am also grateful to Ravi Arora for including me in his book-writing process during my early corporate days, rekindling my childhood dream of becoming an author.

To Manikandan, for handing me the life-changing *Power of Now* in 2016 and helping me find my daily meditation practice, which undoubtedly altered my life's trajectory for the better.

To all my mentors, teachers, and gurus who saw potential in me and helped sculpt me into the person I am today.

To the many authors whose transporting words gave me the courage to dream of an altogether different life—Jiddu Krishnamurti, Osho, Sadhguru, Eckhart Tolle, Virginia Woolf, Maya Angelou, J. K. Rowling, Seneca, and Henry David Thoreau.

To Sria, Trina, Ap, and Mads. I am blessed to have you incredible women in my life. Thank you for sticking by me through countless personal transformations, tolerating my wildly shifting moods, and simply being there whether nearby or oceans apart.

I would be remiss if I didn't convey my heartfelt gratitude to the listeners of the 'Being Meraklis'. podcast, and the early members of the BM Tribe. Your trust and faith in my work gave me the confidence to build 'Being Meraklis'. into something much bigger, paving the way for this book.

A huge shout out to Vikrant Parmar, for his keen eye, sharp insights, and constant guidance to give shape to this manuscript.

Thank you, Hay House India, for believing in my manuscript and helping me share these words with a wider audience. Heartfelt appreciations to my editor Aditya Jarial for refining the manuscript to become this book you hold in your hands. Thank you, Aditya, for your patience and the meaningful edits.

To my entire community of coaches, friends, and well-wishers who continue to believe in me, thank you for the endless support and encouragement.

CONNECT WITH

HAY HOUSE

ONLINE

 hayhouse.co.in

 @hayhouseindia

 @hayhouseindia

 @hayhouseindia

Join the conversation about latest products, events, exclusive offers, contests, giveaways and more.

'The gateways to wisdom and knowledge are always open.'

Louise Hay